THE EFFECTIVENESS OF
IN-SERVICE EDUCATION AND
TRAINING OF TEACHERS AND
SCHOOL LEADERS

EUROPEAN MEETINGS ON EDUCATIONAL RESEARCH

VOLUME 23

Part A
Reports of educational research symposia, colloquies, workshops organised under the auspices of the Council of Europe

Part B
European conferences of directors of educational research institutions organised in cooperation with UNESCO, the UNESCO Institute for Education in Hamburg, and the Council of Europe

UNESCO
UNESCO INSTITUTE FOR EDUCATION — HAMBURG
COUNCIL OF EUROPE — STRASBOURG

The Effectiveness of In-Service Education and Training of Teachers and School Leaders

REPORT OF THE FIFTH ALL-EUROPEAN CONFERENCE
OF DIRECTORS OF EDUCATIONAL RESEARCH INSTITUTIONS
TRIESENBERG (LIECHTENSTEIN) 11-14 OCTOBER 1988

EDITED BY

John Wilson

THE NOTHERN IRELAND COUNCIL
FOR EDUCATIONAL RESEARCH

SWETS & ZEITLINGER B.V. AMSTERDAM / LISSE   1989

SWETS & ZEITLINGER INC. ROCKLAND, MA / BERWYN, PA / PUBLISHING SERVICE /

The points of view, selection of facts and opinions expressed are those of the authors and do not necessarily coincide with the official positions of UNESCO, the UNESCO Institute for Education, Hamburg, or the Council of Europe's Council for Cultural Co-operation.

Library of Congress Cataloging-in-Publication Data
All-European Conference of Directors of Educational Research Institutions (5th : 1988 : Triesenberg, Liechtenstein)
  The effectiveness of in-service education and training of teachers and school leaders : report of the Fifth All-European Conference of Directors of Educational Research Institution, Triesenberg (Liechtenstein) 11-14 October 1988 / edited by John Wilson.
    p.   cm.
  At head of title: UNESCO, UNESCO Institute for Education--Hamburg; Council of Europe--Strasbourg.
  Includes bibliographical references.
  ISBN 902651025X
  1. Teachers--In-service training--Europe--Congresses. 2. School administrators--In-service training--Europe--Congresses. 3. Education-- Research--Europe--Congresses. I. Wilson, John, 1928-. II. Unesco Institute for Education. III Council of Europe. IV. Title.
LB1731.A445 1988
371.1'46--dc20   89-19688
                                                                                                         CIP

CIP-gegevens Koninklijke Bibliotheek, Den Haag

Effectiveness

The effectiveness of in-service education and training of teachers and school leaders : report of the Fifth All-European Conference of Directors of Educational Research Institutions, Triesenberg (Liechtenstein), 11-14 October 1988 / ed. by John Wilson. – Amsterdam [etc.] : Swets & Zeitlinger. – (European meetings on educational research, ISSN 0924-0578 ; 23)
Met lit. opg.
ISBN 90-265-1025-X geb.
SISO 450.4 UDC 371.13 NUGI 724
Trefw.: onderwijsopleidingen

Printed in the Netherlands by Offsetdrukkerij Kanters B.V., Alblasserdam

ISBN 90 265 1025 X   ISSN 0924-0578
NUGI 724

Contents

Preface

The Conference held at Triesenberg in Liechtenstein from 11-14 October 1988 was the fifth in a series of all-European educational research conferences, after Hamburg (1976), Madrid (1979), Neusiedl in Austria (1983) and Eger in Hungary (1986), which involved both the UNESCO Institute for Education (UIE) in Hamburg and the Council for Cultural Co-operation (CCC) of the Council of Europe. For the first time UNESCO in Paris acted as direct organiser as well, and the fourth partner in the organisation was the European Information Centre for Further Education of Teachers, Charles University (Prague). The authorities of the Principality of Liechtenstein acted as hosts to the Conference and made a substantial contribution to its budget.

These conferences have become an important element in the programme of both UIE and the CCC — and now also of UNESCO. European co-operation in educational research aims at providing Ministries of Education with research findings so as to help them to prepare their policy decisions; co-operation should also lead to a joint European evaluation of certain educational reforms. In the case of the Triesenberg Conference the objectives were more precisely:

- to discuss the state of the art in educational research in the European region and to examine ways of strengthening co-operation and co-ordination in this field;
- to take stock of major ongoing, or recently completed, research concerned with the quality and effectiveness of in-service education and training of teachers (INSET);
- to suggest topics for future research in the light of recent trends in INSET and new needs and demands.

The papers of these meetings are in general published as a book so that Ministries and interested research workers as well as a wider public (teachers, parents and the press) are kept informed of the present state of research at the European level.

The Conference at Triesenberg was the result of an initiative by Felix Hassler, member of the Liechtenstein Parliament (having attended the Conference in Hungary in 1986), and Dr Josef Wolf, Head of the Liechtenstein School

Authority, which was gladly accepted by UNESCO, UIE and the CCC. The European Information Centre for Further Education of Teachers in Prague was brought in because of its competence for the chosen theme "The effectiveness of in-service education and training of teachers and leaders", a theme which reflects the current priorities of the organisers as well as of most countries in the European region. The age structure of the teaching body in many countries makes it necessary to focus on INSET rather than on initial teacher education when trying to innovate in schools.

The Conference was attended by research directors and experts from Austria, Belgium, Bulgaria, Canada, Cyprus, Czechoslovakia, Denmark, Finland, France, the Federal Republic of Germany, the German Democratic Republic, Greece, the Holy See, Hungary, Iceland, Ireland, Israel, Italy, Liechtenstein, Luxembourg, Malta, the Netherlands, Norway, Poland, Portugal, San Marino, Spain, Sweden, Switzerland, the United Kingdom, the Ukrainian SSR and Yugoslavia. Albania, the Byelorussian SSR, Romania and Turkey had also been invited. The Parliamentary Assembly of the Council of Europe, OECD, WCOTP, ICET and IEA had sent representatives (see also the list of participants in Appendix 1).

After a keynote address given by Dr Svatopluk Petráček (Czechoslovakia), four commissioned papers summing up research and developments in France, the GDR, the USSR and the United Kingdom were presented in plenary session. These papers were supplemented by a paper from Liechtenstein on experimental language learning with the help of suggestopaedia.

A number of individual or national reports were tabled as background documents and these are listed in Appendix 2 along with the invited papers.

The papers were discussed in four groups, which reported back to the plenary session. Group 1 was chaired by Dr Manfred Haak (GDR), Group 2 by Professor Guy Neave (United Kingdom), Group 3 by Professor Miklos Szabolcsi (Hungary) and Group 4 by Dr Hildegard Pfanner (Austria).

The Rapporteur General, Professor Wolfgang Mitter, summed up the conclusions of the Conference on the morning of the last day.

The conference languages were English, French, Russian and German.

This publication presents only a selection of the Conference papers.

Our thanks are due to the Liechtenstein authorities (in particular Dr Josef Wolf and Dr Bruno Wettstein) for their generous hospitality and help in preparing and organising the Conference, to the European Information Centre for Further Education of Teachers in Prague (Doc. JUDr Svatopluk Petráček, PhDr Marie Černá and PhDr Hana Procházková) for the excellent keynote and background papers written for the Conference and also to the Rapporteur General (Professor Dr Wolfgang Mitter), the lecturers, the group chairmen and group rapporteurs who all made a significant contribution. Our appreciation is also extended to Dr John Wilson from the Northern Ireland Council for Educational Research for editing the manuscript and making it available as camera-ready copy.

Paris/Hamburg/Strasbourg, 23 March 1989

UNESCO   UNESCO Institute   Council of Europe
                      for Education   Strasbourg
                      Hamburg

9

Part 1
Final Report and Commissioned Papers

1

Final Report

Wolfgang Mitter
Rapporteur General
Federal Republic of Germany

1. INTRODUCTION

The organisation of this educational research conference must be regarded as an immediate outcome of the preceding Fourth All-European Conference of Directors of Educational Research Institutions which took place at Eger (Hungary), 13-16 October 1986. At that conference the papers and discussions had laid stress on new challenges for teachers and teacher education, caused by new developments in society, the sciences and the education system itself. When talking about research into teacher education and the identification of shortcomings the teachers' everyday work was given special attention, linked with the question of how their quality and qualifications could be improved. The concept of teacher education underlying that Conference was regarded as overarching, insofar as it comprises both the initial, pre-service and in-service (further) stages, the latter being the focus of particular considerations which can be summarised as follows. We have to start from the experience that, given the dynamics of the sociocultural and economic developments of our time, even teachers who have completed their initial training under optimal conditions have not exhausted their abilities to learn, nor have they ever reached a stage which may allow them to stop their further education. In view of the continuity of this process, teacher education, and in this case in-service training, is embedded in the overall postulate of lifelong education.

It was this general assumption which led the organising institutions to the decision to devote a special conference to in-service training (INSET), its objectives, procedures, organisational patterns, deficits and postulates. This Conference has underlined the need for such a special discussion, the more so as the plenary speakers as well as many participants made clear, and as Michael Eraut stated in an exemplary way, that "the field of in-service education has not been widely or deeply researched". There was wide agreement that this observation must be given serious consideration, although it seems to be questioned by the availability of voluminous bibliographies. Most publications, it was repeatedly pointed out, remained either at the level of general and abstract conceptualisation or were restricted to descriptive presentations, lacking in in-depth quality.

Let me make a few general comments in order to indicate the peculiar nature of this Conference. Compared with the preceding four conferences, this Conference was particularly characterised by its approximation to the needs of everyday teaching practice, and that in two aspects:

— the identification of deficits in research,
— the plea for clarifying the teacher's real needs.

Due to these basic considerations, the plenary speakers focussed their analyses on experiences in their respective countries and on the presentation of postulates directly derived from the observation of grassroot deficiencies. In this way their papers, on the one hand, reflected specific problems related to national education systems, while, on the other hand, they were composed as components of an all-European panorama of experiences, problems, outlooks and postulates. This was the specific impression one got from studying the papers, listening to the author's clarifying comments, and afterwards from participating in the discussions.

These basic considerations emerged in the introductory addresses, whose speakers underlined them by referring to the Conferences of Minister of Education in Helsinki (1987) and Paris (1988) and by expressing their expectations of this Conference. JOSEF WOLF, in his capacity as host of this Conference, emphasised the advisory and evaluating function of educational research. ETIENNE BRUNSWICK, in transmitting the best wishes of the Director General of UNESCO, underlined this issue and paid special attention to the need to overcome difficulties in communicating research findings to policymakers and practitioners. MAITLAND STOBART, in bringing the greetings of the Secretary General of the Council of Europe, examined the demand for research in the light of ongoing changes in society and, in particular, he pointed to the widely neglected issue of procedures for the selection of candidates for admission to teacher training and for the selection of teacher trainers.

Finally, RAVINDRA DAVE, in drafting the programme and structure of this Conference, identified the following three questions with which the deliberations should begin:

(a) what are the goals and tasks of this Conference?
(b) what measures have been taken and what programmes have been organised to achieve these goals?
(c) what are the major elements and focal points in the in-service training of teachers?

His answer to question (c) crystallised into the statement that INSET must be regarded as a process aimed at updating "professional preparedness for maintaining and improving the duality of teaching and learning".

2. THE PLENARY PAPERS

Since the plenary papers will be published in full, I feel able to concentrate on a few of the focal topics and issues the speakers dealt with, particularly in the light of their oral comments.

SVATOPLUK PETRÁČEK, in his keynote address, gave a state-of-the-art account of INSET and, in particular, of research and evaluation in this field. After underlining the changing requirements imposed on teachers' qualifications by socioeconomic and cultural developments and by the progress of educational sciences, he gave an outline of organisational differences among the national INSET systems. He drew attention to the role of teachers and administrators in those systems and in particular to the factors influencing the concept and its underlying situation under various national, cultural and social conditions. Particular weight was assigned to the standards of teacher trainers in regard to their functional diversification as:

(a) permanent members of INSET institutions,
(b) university teachers,
(c) master teachers (in their capacity as models for other teachers),
(d) inspectors.

In his further presentation Petráček emphasised the deficiencies in INSET programmes and identified specific needs, with special regard to the "induction training of new teachers" and "teachers' motivation for INSET". As regards models of INSET he made a fundamental distinction between organisation-oriented models and models based on the example of teachers "who are expected to take the initiative for their own self-induction". Though clearly stressing the deficits of research, Petráček, in his general outlook, projected an optimistic picture of INSET, referring to the growing awareness in society of the changing role of the teacher in the light of the new challenges which had been discussed at Eger. It should be added that this positive outlook — in its overall orientation — differed from the rather cautious, if not sceptical, comments made by other plenary speakers and discussants.

Finally, Petráček pointed to new challenges pertaining to the contents of INSET in all societies regardless of their political constitutions or orientations:

— education for international understanding, co-operation and peace,
— education related to human rights, fundamental freedoms and rights of nations,
— environmental education,
— education in information technology,
— health education (in particular struggle against disease, drug abuse, alcohol and AIDS),
— media education.

MICHAEL ERAUT's concept of INSET covered all activities aimed at improving the teacher's knowledge and abilities. That is to say that "INSET has to take into account all occasions and situations where teacher learning occurs". Consequently he posed four "fundamental questions" in regard of

— INSET needs,
— knowledge to be learned,
— the relations between such knowledge and ongoing practice,
— facilitating and inhibiting factors.

As for needs' assessment, which he thoroughly discussed, Eraut gave three actual examples demonstrating cases where educational policies fell short of expected success because of neglecting the basic task of making teachers aware of the changes to be achieved by their actions. To call the reader's special attention to what he laid stress on, let me also underline his taking "the notion of the pupil as the ultimate client'' of needs' assessment: "Any statement of the teacher's needs or school needs is predicated on some view of what teachers should be doing for their pupils''.

Further attention should be directed to Eraut's defining three types of knowledge which, according to his analysis, constitute the purpose of INSET:

(a)   subject knowledge,
(b)   education knowledge,
(c)   societal knowledge.

This categorisation had proved, he said, to be highly applicable, insofar as it corresponded to the working spaces the teacher is assigned to, i.e. the classroom, the school and the social environment. On the other hand, these types of knowledge must be imparted according to how they are likely to be used, as:

(a)   classroom knowledge,
(b)   classroom-related knowledge,
(c)   management knowledge,
(d)   other professional knowledge,
(e)   purely personal knowledge.

Special mention, he emphasised, must be made of the importance of societal knowledge, because it had been most neglected in teacher preservice education as well as in INSET.

Traditional research methods, Eraut concluded, were insufficient as a means of identifying teaching assets and deficiencies. This difficulty arose from a fundamental complexity whereby teachers' practical experience and intuitive knowledge crystallises into "implicit theories". In order to optimise INSET, approaches must be used which reach classroom training and staff development.

VIKTOR ONUSHKIN gave an insight into the efforts to develop research on INSET in the Soviet Union, which is centred at the Research Institute of General Adult Education at the Academy of Pedagogical Sciences of the USSR. This research was embedded, he pointed out in detail, in the current educational reforms directed to establishing a consistent and uninterrupted stream of schooling for all youngsters and adults. Research on INSET, he continued, had to be focussed on these two tasks:

(a) to give instruction and advice to teachers,
(b) to invest energies in developing the teacher's personal capacities and creative potential.

One could easily make out that Onushkin gave priority to the second task to be tackled as the essential contribution to promoting the teacher's "professional growth". His defining the teacher's role in INSET "as a free, equal and responsible participant in the system of collective interpersonal relationships" is worth emphasising.

In his concluding remarks Onushkin raised some crucial methodological questions. In doing so he devoted particular attention to how to establish an optimal equilibrium between quantitative and qualitative procedures and between the search for objectivity in the process and outcome of evaluative inquiry and the "subjective moment" which must be accepted as an unavoidable component.

In his paper HELMUT STOLZ presented a survey of the extensive research programme dealing with further education of teachers in the German Democratic Republic since the seventies. In his account of the content of further education which has been developed and evaluated, one could discover certain similarities to Michael Eraut's categorisation. These were seen in how the guidelines of the research project, "The content and choice of further education", were defined, in particular with regard to investigating the teacher's personal development and the transmission of professional and pedagogical knowledge.

In his oral presentation he picked up some relevant practical issues, such as:

(a) the confirmation of Michael Eraut's statement that the greater part of INSET takes place in the schools;
(b) the reading preferences of teachers for literature which directly affects their everyday work at the cost of theoretical and methodological publications;
(c) the importance of experience in INSET, thus, again, reinforcing Eraut's findings;
(d) the contents of INSET, with special regard to the inclusion of research on medical and psychological issues;
(e) finally, the steps which have been taken in the German Democratic Republic to qualify and engage specially trained advisory teachers.

Stolz concluded by stressing the need for assessing the following three factors in INSET:

(1) the degree of satisfaction among participants of courses etc.,
(2) their motivation and the degree of their preparedness for engaging themselves in INSET programmes,
(3) the degree and quality of behavioural change as the most relevant factor in raising teachers' professional competencies.

FRANCINE VANISCOTE, in interpreting the paper which had been prepared by Francine Best and Monique Vial, illustrated the situation of INSET research in France. In particular the authors of this paper emphasised the need for "prospective research" and provided information on the useful experience which had been gained from the success of projects based on action research. Another interesting item dealt with the benefit young teachers could gain from attending courses addressed to "animateurs" in the areas of holiday and leisure. These activities, however, should not replace the traditional forms of five-day courses or seminars.

RUDOLF BATLINER's contribution introduced an alternative dimension into the Conference, insofar as he gave an insight into the remarkable efforts of a small country, namely the Principality of Liechtenstein, to organise an efficient education system and, in particular, to recognise the importance of initial and in-service teacher training as part of the over-arching educational task. INSET in Liechtenstein, as Batliner described in detail, is focussed on "suggestopaedia". He defined it as a "teaching-learning method which combined didactic principles known for a long time with some more recent findings from education and neuropsychology". According to George Lozanov's concept, suggestopaedia is aimed at liberating "the personality of the pupil from the unnatural restraint of norms established by society". Stimulated by the speaker's questions, several participants pointed to ongoing experiments with "suggestopaedia" in their own countries.

All the plenary speakers concluded their presentations by identifying specific questions or issues for discussion which concentrated on the need to improve INSET and to promote research in both a national and international context. The actuality of these postulates was reinforced by the remarkable number of reports dealing with the state of the art in European countries or describing individual projects and their outcomes.

Moreover, valuable information had been provided by the European Information Centre of the Charles University for Further Education of Teachers in Prague and special mention must be made on the following two papers because of their informative and analytical quality:

— "Comparative analysis of the information process in the field of in-service training of educational personnel", submitted by Hana Prochazkova, Jitka Hradilova and Anna Souckova;
— comparative report "In-service training of teachers in the eighties", submitted by Marie Cerna.

3. COMPARATIVE CONSIDERATIONS

Without claiming to make any attempt at completeness, the following considerations represent an attempt to identify some essential problems which were given special attention in the discussions which were stimulated by the plenary speakers' presentations. It is true that the participants' focal interest pertained to the role research has to play in improving INSET. However, the deficits in this area, which I mentioned already, may be considered as the essential reason why many interventions immediately resulted in the formulation of postulates on the one hand and the highlighting of crucial issues concerning INSET itself on the other.

I do not feel like duplicating the reports which the groups presented. Instead, it has seemed to me reasonable to choose five main criteria on which to base my comments. Needless to say, I shall try to concentrate on tackling questions which give insight into needs which are common to all countries or, to be more correct, which are similar to each other. Let me also offer my overall impression that the discussions in the four working groups were rich in illustrating reports on individual cases. These are the criteria on which I shall sum up my observations, being well aware of the subjective bias in my presentation, which is therefore more of a "comment" than a "report" in the proper sense:

(1) aims of INSET,
(2) working conditions,
(3) responsibility structures,
(4) didactic approaches,
(5) further education as a factor in the teacher's career.

In an additional approach some attention should be paid to the headteacher's role in INSET and to the teacher trainers' education as well as to the methodological aspects of research on INSET.

3.1 Aims of INSET

In comparing the systems of further education of teachers within the framework of national societies, one has to be aware of a remarkable diversity, as regards the formulation of aims and objectives in national documents of an official and non-official character. The discussions have made clear that, as the extent of this diversity increases, the more the objectives come near the level of concrete needs and requirements. However, it was also pointed out that empirical evidence had shown a high degree of congruity in over-arching national aims, which should not be surprising in view of the global societal changes which had been tackled at Eger. In general, the interventions were related to the following aims which dominated the discussion:

(a) most frequently emphasised was that of qualitative improvement in the professional abilities and skills of teachers. There are various objectives to be derived from the aim to improve quality. They can be subsumed by the extension of scientific and didactic knowledge and the corresponding professional skills teachers need in their capacity as agents of knowledge transfer and producers of new knowledge. In this context we should be reminded of the systematised schemes concerning knowledge patterns and levels to be imparted in in-service training, as were presented by Michael Eraut and Helmut Stolz;

(b) further reference was made to a second group of objectives consisting of pedagogical, psychological, and sociological components aimed at enabling teachers to communicate with their pupils;

(c) the third group, closely related to the second, was identified as a means pertaining to all competencies teachers must possess in coping with the "school" and the "social environment" beyond the "classroom";

(d) beside the "school-oriented" aims (in the narrow sense of this term) reference, though to rather a small extent, was made to the aim comprising all the objectives which are directed to the teacher's role as change agent in the education system. Let me only select one point in this context, namely the school-parent relationship as realising the fundamental role parents play as their children's educators in all European countries. Irrespective of their constitutional, ideological and legal conditions, it is

21

astonishing how little weight has been assigned to making teachers aware of handling co-operation with parents. Eraut's following remark can be quoted as typical of this deficiency: ''At no time have school-parent relations been identified as a major INSET need for all schools. In my view this has been a mistake'';

(e)   finally, there seemed to be wide consensus about the aim to develop and strengthen the teacher's "creative potential", to return to Viktor Onushkin's deliberate argumentation. However, one also learned that it is just this aim which needs to be subjected to further clarifying work, the more so as it necessarily includes the sphere of individual and societal value systems and orientations.

3.2 Working conditions of INSET

Viktor Onushkin and Helmut Stolz provided exemplary information by recording that teachers in most socialist countries of Eastern Europe are obliged to attend, on a regular basis, organised in-service training courses and to participate in school-based further education activities. Most West European policy-makers, however, have up to now refrained from making such attendance mandatory. Taking this problem as a whole, there certainly is a tension to cope with, as came distinctly out of the French plenary paper. From a comparative point of view, the apparent dichotomy between the teacher's need to continuously update his or her qualifications and the absence of mandatory requirements is caused, in part, by budgetary concerns. Making further training in organised forms mandatory compels legislative bodies at various levels to provide additional financial means. Furthermore there exists, as it was repeatedly argued, a deeper problem which concerns the self-awareness and social status of teachers as mediators of civic and moral values in democratic societies. As a corollary of the respective discussions the idea has gained ground that further education should be regarded as an essential component of what is called the "teacher's autonomy".

Taken together, both factors support the explanation of why most governments and school authorities in Western Europe prefer to rely on the effect of appeals or recommendations. However, the observation that INSET does not reach those teachers who need it most urgently has led to proposals and, in some cases, even legal initiatives comprising mandatory INSET requirements, whereas some socialist countries tend to broaden the optional component without cancelling the mandatory nucleus.

In a number of countries, debates about the range of the "teacher's autonomy" have affected the competence and organisation of school inspection. The international spectrum has revealed a certain trend from supervisory to advisory forms of inspection, apart from the further innovation of introducing the particular function of "advisory teachers".

3.3 Responsibility structures

The importance of this criterion, as it emerged in various interventions, is shown by the experience that the responsibility structure for educational policy directly affects conceptualisation, planning, and organisation of INSET programmes. Let me try to synthesise the respective interventions by rendering the following reflections:

(a) as regards responsibility for INSET, there are countries where the Ministry of Education is the active initiator of programmes and projects in the education system and this variant covers the majority of European countries. Under this condition, INSET is clearly considered as an instrument of overall national policies, initiated and conducted by the steering agencies formed by central institutions which are grouped round the Ministry of Education. At the opposite end of the spectrum we find those initiatives which take place at the "grassroots" level in individual schools or local communities. Between the "initiatives from above" and the "initiatives at the grassroots", diverse arrangements at regional levels are placed. Whether these "intermediate" agencies mainly reinforce national policies, or are orientated toward supporting local innovations, depends again on the given overall responsibility structure. In this context surprise was raised by the information about the high degree of decentralisation in France, which Francine Vaniscote presented as a "paradoxical" phenomenon with regard to the centralised structure of the French education system as a whole;

(b) there is, of course, a close correlation between the responsibility structure and the institutional models. Whereas centralised educational agencies, such as Ministries of Education, tend to establish and maintain specific governmental institutes for in-service training, education systems with grassroots-oriented initiatives prefer local arrangements, as well as school-based INSET activities. However, there was wide agreement that this form of INSET innovation has recently gained increasing support in many countries, regardless of their political systems and administrative structures. The discussions resulted in statements to the effect that on the

23

European scene as a whole there is a trend toward mixed responsibility systems responding to specific objectives, tasks and situations. On the one hand, there is a growing need for participation of all the persons and groups directly concerned with innovations, i.e. first of all, teachers, but also parents and agents of the local communities, as well as pupils. On the other hand, rapid changes at the superordinate societal level underline the need for agencies which are able to implement nation-wide or, to a growing degree, even region-wide reforms;

(c)   this Conference concentrated on INSET programmes initiated by public agencies, irrespective of their central, regional or local status. However, this did not mean ignoring the variegated initiatives in some countries which take place in the "private" sector, this term being used in its widest sense as opposed to "public". There are two societal agencies worth taking into explicit account: on the one hand teacher unions and associations, on the other churches or their associate agencies. Both of them organise INSET programmes for teachers in a good number of countries, often in centres of adult education, and they also take part in the formulation and implementation of public training programmes, as is the particular case in the Netherlands and also, though to a lesser degree, in the Federal Republic of Germany.

3.4 Didactic approaches

It should not cause any astonishment that didactic approaches were discussed most thoroughly. Michael Eraut, in commenting on his paper, had paved the way for considering this criterion by formulating the following three questions related to the teacher's profession: "What do teachers learn?", "How do they learn?" and "How could they learn?", given adequate learning opportunities. Several discussants joined the speaker in his plea for recognising the importance of the last two questions, thereby demonstrating the priority of "process"-orientation in INSET over the hitherto dominating "product"-orientation.

The "classical method" in INSET has been the lecture, which still prevails in the courses which are organised by central institutions and also by teacher training colleges or universities. Several case reports revealed that nowadays in many "innovatory models" lectures are enriched by seminars and working groups which, however, often prove to be an extension of the lecturer's demonstration, thereby limiting the teacher's role to that of a passive "trainee". This observation is particularly true of courses which are run by university or college teachers. Irrespective of their scientific competence, which may be beyond doubt, they are often lacking interactive abilities, which unequivocally raises the question of how to train the "trainers".

On the other hand, cases were recorded which illustrated recent efforts to break the monopoly of "formal" lectures and seminars. In general, these aim at including the participating teachers in the planning and implementation of their further education activities. The success of this alternative approach, however, greatly depends on the interactive abilities of trainers and trainees, on the openness of the dialogue, and on the provision of feed-back cycles to give teachers the chance of evaluating the efficiency of their in-service training activities in respect of their teaching practice. Promising alternative approaches have been made in workshop programmes and in the multifarious opportunities offered to school-based initiatives.

Though not congruent in their appraisals, speakers and participants widely agreed that one should beware of one-sided solutions. Let me quote Helmut Stolz in this context: "Exercises in the 'normal' seminars are essentially more broadly effective, but do not lead to the changes in the abilities of individual teachers.... Thus, in further education the main attention must be directed to increasing those parts of the seminar which exercise abilities in order to make the seminars more effective".

3.5 Further education as a factor in the teacher's career
It is true that INSET must be regarded as an essential component in the teacher's professional task. It was suggested, however, that it is just the tension between the mandatory and voluntary qualities of teachers' engagement in INSET that leads to the search for "additional" incentives. In this respect career-promotion by successful participation in organised INSET programmes can certainly be regarded as an issue to be taken into serious consideration, as it is expressed by the West German concept of "Weiterbildung". This point was not widely tackled at this Conference but it seemed that it should not be missing from the list of synthesising criteria.

3.6 Headteachers and teacher trainers
The important role of the headteacher as an initiator of school-based INSET activities and, generally speaking, as a stimulating force for in-service training was emphasised in a number of interventions and in the formulation of desiderata. In particular, reference has to be made to the presentations of Viktor Onushkin and Helmut Stolz. However, the question of how to prepare

headteachers for this special task and, in general, for their specific professional duties, seems to have been somewhat neglected at this Conference. In this respect one should pay attention to current efforts brought about by the experience that in modern societies effective headteachers cannot just rely on their former "good" teaching practice when taking over their new functions in the school. In this context Eraut's reference to the need for "management knowledge" gains its special importance.

Some discussants, finally, drew attention to an essential deficiency concerning both initial and in-service training, namely the training of teacher trainers. It must be identified with special regard to the fact that, in many countries, teacher trainers are appointed only on the basis of their academic careers, which are often totally lacking in school experience. Of course, this observation mainly concerns secondary teacher training and INSET. However, since in a number of countries the training of primary school teachers has been transferred to universities, the problem has reached a wider dimension. It was added that this overall deficit is often aggravated by the fact that lecturers are not familiar with their trainees' everyday problems.

3.7 Methodological aspects of research in INSET

Following the appraisals and suggestions which had been put forward by all the plenary speakers, the working groups underlined the linkage between the identification of themes, as dealt with in the preceding sections, and the development of adequate methods as the key question concerning research on INSET.

The importance of qualitative methods, to be achieved by ethnographic approaches, non-standardised interviews and case studies, was repeatedly emphasised. In this context the various reports and proposals dealing with the inclusion of teachers in research programmes in the form of action research (in the widest sense of this term) must be regarded as an important innovatory step. This innovation, it was intimated, is not easy to achieve, since it necessitates special training programmes devoted to introducing teachers to research theories and, above all, to research methods.

On the other hand, several speakers made clear that "traditional" quantitative methods must not be abandoned. INSET was identified as a thematic field of research, waiting for controlled experimentation and involving the application of different methods.

4. CHALLENGES AND OBSTACLES

The variety of different projects which have been initiated in many European countries at the national, regional, and local levels bear witness to growing insights into the need for the further education of teachers. Moreover, this Conference gave evidence of new challenges which underline and reinforce this need:

(a) the spread of new technologies into the classroom cannot be just added on to the existing requirements serving teachers have to tackle in the course of their professional work. Computers, in particular micro-computers, not only make them acquire new knowledge and skills, but put them in the learning situation of "professional beginners". In acquiring computer literacy teachers often find themselves in a position where they have to compete with their own pupils, in regard not only to learning speed, but also to the ability to use imagination and creativity. Besides, in this context one must not neglect the problems which are posed by the "older" technologies, represented by the media (radio, TV, and video). Educating children how to use the media and evaluate the transmitted programmes in a mind-promoting (and not mind-disturbing) way was identified as another essential component of INSET;

(b) considering the dynamic nature of the technological, economic and social development humankind is involved in, the task of being a change agent in the capacity of teacher, educator and social worker demands creativity and flexibility on his/her part in all his/her professional considerations and actions to an extent former generations could have only dreamed of. Several discussants pointed to the empirical finding that most teachers tend to be rather conservative people. Any alternative aiming at a total revolution of teachers' attitudes in favour of "progressive" trends is certainly not desirable, because education and upbringing need "conservative" qualities as well. Nevertheless it was argued that further education must lay stress on maintaining, developing, and re-awakening the teachers' steady readiness to cope with emerging and changing challenges. This task is aggravated by the need to encourage the commitment of teachers to the challenges of peace, environmental and health education; otherwise there is a danger of these issues remaining at the declamatory level and causing indifferent or even cynical attitudes among pupils instead of making them aware of the need to positively respond to those challenges;

(c) teaching and educating in classroom and school have always profited from the continuous entry of young teachers who feed the school with new knowledge, skills and ideas. As a result of declining birth-rates and budgetary cuts schools in a number of countries have more and more closed their doors to young qualified applicants. Apart from considerable unemployment among holders of teachers' diplomas as an evil in itself which is reinforced by their "emigration" to other professional fields, schools have to face the trend of "ageing" staffs, as Maitland Stobart observed. This emergency proves to be a new challenge to further education, insofar as it becomes the responsible agency for laying the institutionalised ground for the improvement of school education, while lacking the direct contribution of initial teacher training to fulfilling this task.

As regards obstacles to improving INSET, the critical remarks made by Francine Best and Monique Vial in their paper should be noted in this context. Indifference or even reluctance among decision-makers in educational policy and administration as well as among representatives of the "classical" university disciplines is certainly not a phenomenon limited to France. It can be made out as a world-wide or, with regard to this conference, as a Europe-wide problem. "Professionalisation" of teacher training, therefore, is still widely conceived as a task which can be restricted to the conveyance of "subject knowledge" for classroom use, to quote Michael Eraut again.

The dualism in teacher education, also criticised by Francine Best and Monique Vial, proves to be another obstacle to developing reasonable INSET structures. It includes the danger of narrowing teachers' professional awareness to the type of school where they teach and of blocking their openness to the task of education and upbringing as a whole, never mind their understanding of the "world outside" and in particular the world of work and the sociopolitical environment. The initiation of common INSET projects to include teachers of different school types and stages is, therefore, worth identifying as a an item on the list of innovatory needs.

5. CONCLUDING REMARKS

Let me conclude by putting forward some personal remarks. The Fifth All-European Conference of Directors of Educational Research Institutions has certainly resulted in the identification of a great number of reasonable and stimulating observations, arguments and postulates. It seems that the degree of linkage between educational practice, in this context INSET practice, and the urgent demand for research has been both remarkable and more fully articulated than in previous conferences.

This asset, as it seems, may be traced back on the one hand to the particular interdependence between the two sides of one model. On the other hand it signalises consistent planning on the part of the organising persons and agencies, taking into special consideration the organisation of this Conference as a follow-up meeting of the Fourth Conference which gave speakers and participants the opportunity to enter *in medias res* without having to tackle time-consuming issues of general socioeconomic and political concern. This favourable approach also created an awareness, from a comparative background, of the existence of All-European essentials and the need to harmonise avoidable differences. It also ensured an acknowledgement of that diversity of concepts, methods and operations which bear witness to the ongoing inclusion of education in superordinate sociocultural processes and their national peculiarities. This dialectic tension was underlined by the panel discussion dealing with overall topical issues in educational research.

The postulate, to translate valuable proposals made at this Conference into joint projects of international scope, as expressed and supported by several speakers, remains on the agenda. Due to budgetary reasons and, moreover, to the dependence of most national research institutions on their governmental decision-makers, it seems, however, to be unrealistic to restrict this postulate to the goodwill of the research institutions concerned. Support by national and international authorities and/or other sponsoring agencies — in the form of grants and legal provisions — is urgently needed.

Contrary to predictions which have been made by the "deschoolers" and their adherents, schools have proved their position as vital institutions in our time. At the end of the 1980s it seems that there are no signs indicating their disappearance. Taking this view, we are fully aware of the impact of the "traditional" demands as well as of the new challenges to teacher education and, in particular, to inservice-training and the necessity to conduct research in this field.

There is ample empirical evidence confirming the actuality of the following words of the German educationist Friedrich Diesterweg almost 125 years ago, including the implicit inclusion of INSET: "The school is worth precisely what the teacher is worth and for this reason an improvement in teacher education is a first step in any educational reform."

2
Meeting the Challenges of the Nineties

Trends in In-Service Education and Training (INSET) of Educational Personnel

Svatopluk Petráček
Keynote Speaker
Czechoslovakia

1. INTRODUCTION

Within the topic of this keynote paper I would like to raise some ideas on the in-service education and training (INSET) of educational personnel, as they have developed through the last decade, and suggest their significance for the nineties.

First of all, let me briefly characterise how far we have progressed in the field of in-service training of educational personnel in the European region. Then I shall say a few words on anticipated further developments in this field.

2. PAST DEVELOPMENTS AND PRESENT STATE OF AFFAIRS

It is an established fact that, within the general concept of the lifelong education of teachers and other educational personnel, as characterised by their pre-service and in-service training, comprehensive and systematic attention if being devoted to the improvement of INSET for teachers and other educational personnel, having regard to the particular socio-economic conditions and possibilities of each individual European country.

Very few fields in the development of educational systems have been exposed to so deep an analysis in the last few years as that of INSET for teachers and other educational personnel — for the sake of brevity I shall henceforth refer to them only as teachers.

2.1 Available Material
For instance, we have at our disposal a detailed analysis of the issues of staff/ faculty development in the European region, as submitted for discussion at the Prague Seminar of Unesco experts on staff development in higher education, representing individual countries of the European region (Prague, 1985). Also available are the studies on the stage of development of INSET in the socialist countries, presented at the international seminar in Vietnam (Tmej, 1985). There exists extensive analytical and synthetical material on INSET, worked out by the OECD (Hopkins, 1986) and an extensive comparative study initiated by Unesco on INSET for teachers in Europe, prepared by an international team of specialists (Hoeben, 1986). We have the report on *Tomorrow's Teachers* from the USA (Holmes, 1986) and an excellent analysis of INSET in the 12 member states of the European Community, a study initiated by the Commission of the European Community (Blackburn and Moisan, 1987). We have also a document on INSET worked out within the framework of the Council of Europe for the Conference of European Ministers of Education (Helsinki, 1987) and numerous materials from the events organised annually by such non-governmental organisations as ICET (Yff, 1983), which have given priority attention, *inter alia*, to issues of INSET. Last but not least, there are the resources for information disseminated from Unesco IBE and the European Information Centre for Further Education of Teachers, Charles University, Prague.

2.2 General trends in the last decade
What are the general trends that have characterised the development of INSET of teachers in Europe in the last decade?

INSET as a priority. First of all, it can be stated that in-service training of teachers in all countries of the European region is now being considered a fundamental factor for the improvement of the educational process in all forms and types of educational activity. All governments are aware of the importance of INSET and devote much attention to raising its quality. Despite the fact that individual European countries conceive INSET in different ways, they always proceed from the educational principle — verified in both theory and practice — that the teacher is an irreplaceable agent of the educational process at all levels of the education system and in all types of educational provision. Another acknowledged principle is that the quality of education depends decisively on the quality of the teacher's personality as well as on the quality of the teaching. It follows that a teacher is only able to fulfil his or her educational duties when he or she is both well prepared for the profession and able to improve his or her skills through lifelong education.

Governments allocate considerable sums to INSET from state budgets; new organisational structures are being established, co-ordinating the pre-service training and INSET of teachers on the one hand, and INSET training itself on the other. It is also a fact that numerous initiatives in this field are still in their infancy or have to cope with a vast number of problems. In no case, for various reasons, have INSET systems in all countries reached the optimum level or fulfilled the demands put on them by the development of society.

INSET concepts. Where INSET is effective it provides answers to the following questions:

    — what are the reasons for organising INSET?
    — what are the main objectives and issues of organised INSET?

Both questions are interrelated. The question of "why INSET systems are organised for teachers" governs decisions on their objectives and their target groups. The answers concerning the objectives and the target groups provide answers as to why INSET is organised.

INSET systems for teachers tend to meet, first of all, the following challenges:

    — the changing requirements imposed by socio-economic and cultural development on educational systems, teachers and other educational personnel;

33

— the changing requirements imposed on teacher's qualifications by the educational sciences and improvements in the level of performance of the teaching profession.

It is also evident that, besides specific social needs, the concepts of INSET are under the influence of many other stimuli which cannot be ignored. Thus, for example, INSET is influenced by the changing needs and aspirations of students, by the experience gained by the teacher from the beginning of his or her career, by the sum of the teacher's experience in relation to the improvement of subject specialisation, by the outcomes of the teacher's self-education and by the results of self-critical professional assessment.

Significant differences exist in the organisation of INSET systems. On the one hand there is a considerable diversity and connected with it the seeking of clear communication links and a certain unity of action. On the other hand, these systems are integrated in overall educational systems (especially in the socialist countries). In this respect there arises the question of the range of INSET and the implementation of its general concept within teachers' lifelong education.

Because of its variety, it is difficult to generalise with regard to the purposes, forms, methods and levels of INSET. There is agreement, however, on the following aspects: a growing interest in finding suitable forms of INSET; the inability of existing systems fully to satisfy the needs of society in this field; a keen interest in, and much activity devoted to, improving the quality of INSET within the context of lifelong education.

Role of teachers and school administrators in INSET. Considerable attention is also being paid to the clarification of the role that should be assumed by teachers and social administrators in INSET. These efforts should lead to the creation of new, viable concepts for INSET. Specific measures are therefore called for to assist the teacher in adapting to changes resulting from political, socio-economic and cultural development, each of which brings new requirements for the teaching profession, the formation of the teacher's attitude and the improvement of the national educational system.

In the process of clarifying the concept of INSET several factors influence the situation to varying degrees, depending on the national context. These include the moral involvement of teachers, the level of co-ordination between pre-service and in-service training, the significance attached to individual courses, the administrative and legal regulations in force in the field of education in the respective countries, the attitudes and opinions of those who carry out INSET and the teachers' attitudes towards the concept of INSET and their role in its implementation.

Standards of teacher trainers. The key problem in promoting a considerable improvement in the quality of INSET is that of how to increase the professional competence of the teacher trainers who are involved in INSET courses. Efforts areaimed at creating conditions under which the greatest possible number of teachers can participate in INSET. This should be by ensuring that the organised programmes are stimulating and relevant, since their quality depends, to a decisive extent, on those who deliver lectures and organise the programmes. Therefore adequate attention must be devoted to the pre-service and in-service training of those teacher trainers responsible for INSET, be it teachers working permanently in teacher training institutions, university teachers who deal with the issues of INSET within their educational research, or master teachers who, through their attitudes and performance, have become models for others, and last but not least inspectors.

The problem of resources. A significant part of the analyses of the situation in the field of INSET has been devoted to the resources necessary for the effective functioning of the INSET system. It concerns mainly the financial, material and information components of the system. This problem area is quite extensive; it differs from one country to another and depends on many factors (for example, whether INSET is compulsory or not; whether it is carried out within working hours, whether participation fees are covered by the employer etc.).

Role of school leaders. In the course of raising the quality of INSET considerable attention is paid to the role of school principals. It has become apparent that in the early stages of INSET their key role in the implementation of the concept was under-estimated. The latest development in this field shows growing efforts to recognise fully the principal's irreplaceable role in the process of INSET. His or her fundamental duties include the help offered to teachers at the school level in developing their knowledge and skills, using the well-established forms of school-based INSET. This mainly concerns the need to stimulate the exchange of theoretical knowledge and practical experience as well as the use of contacts among teachers themselves and their contacts with the out-of-school environment (parents, public officials, authorities, future employers of school graduates etc.). Another characteristic feature of the principal's activity is the art of combining the development of the school with the teachers' needs on the basis of a long-term perspective of the needs of the school, and to respect those needs in the course of conceiving the organisation and content of INSET. The one important lesson is the necessity to avoid, as far as possible, those courses the concept of which could only satisfy the short-term needs of the school.

Effectiveness of INSET. Considerable attention has been devoted to the evaluation of the effectiveness of INSET without, however, achieving any remarkable results. It has become apparent that clearly defined objectives for such evaluation have not been set, nor does there exist any reliable assessment methodology. Even though we have witnessed numerous attempts at establishing such a methodology of assessment, the results achieved do not have sufficient value. However, this does not mean that methods for the assessment of INSET programmes could not be devised, for example, by a group of course participants or by a group of teachers organising and carrying out the courses and using methods of work evaluation in the classroom.

Induction training of new teachers. The induction training of new teachers has become a matter of interest to many specialists and numerous positive results have been achieved in this respect. However, it is necessary to point out that the induction period is not everywhere integrated into the INSET system. It still remains the last phase of teacher education.

Nevertheless, as regards the organisational allegiance of induction training, there still are a number of open questions on the mutual relation between the training of the teacher and his or her induction training. In the socialist countries the induction training of the teacher is the first stage within the INSET system (In this respect it is necessary to take into account that the student teachers undergo their initial teaching practice within the four to five years of college or university training).

Teachers' motivation for INSET. All systems of INSET face the problem of how to arouse the interest of a greater number of teachers. Connected with this is also the problem of the involvement of excellent teachers, for their involvement gives a guarantee for raising the efficiency of INSET. Analyses have shown that those forms of INSET in which the teachers themselves help to determine their needs, or those which are an expression of the collective standpoint of the respective educational staff, are most successful. In the course of planning INSET, thoughtful organisers respect the developmental needs of the school while having regard also to the needs expressed by the teachers themselves or the educational staff.

INSET co-ordination. At present the question of INSET, in its broadest sense, is the main concern of discussions on the development of educational systems at the international level. It has attracted the attention of numerous national and international professional groups and organisations with widely different interests. This has resulted in the need to improve the co-ordination of national, regional and international activities and their subordination to a clear general concept of INSET in the context of lifelong education — involving teachers' recruitment, their pre-service training, and including all types of INSET in accordance with the educational poiicy of each country and taking into account accepted international standards and recommendations.

The activities of Unesco and its specialised organisations, the International Bureau of Education (IBE) and the Unesco Institute of Education in Hamburg, have been powerful stimuli for the intensification of international co-operation in this field.

INSET objectives, structures and models. The majority of *INSET objectives* has been oriented to personality and behavioural change in order to meet require-ments imposed by the development of society, the economy and culture upon the educational system, including the teachers. Consequently, from the psychological point of view, it means changes in attitudes. The level of these changes influences all the functions of INSET, including compensation (filling gaps in the teacher's qualification), adaptation (attending to the needs of the beginning teacher through induction training), requalification (bridging the gap between the original qualification and new requirements imposed upon the teacher), extension (acquiring the competence to teach an additional subject), specialisation (providing the teacher with the possibility of acquiring a supple-mentary qualification, e.g. specialisation in educational technology) and inno-vation (training as creating the necessary link between educational theory and educational practice, between projected reforms and their implementation).

Apart from the principal functions presented above, INSET is characterised by many other features which have come to light only recently. Thus, for example, it promotes better contacts between teachers and encourages the exchange of experience; it provides the opportunity for visiting other places, mainly cities. The fact that for a limited period the teachers become students allows them to get rid of the tendency towards stereotyping, dogmatism and authoritarianism, and increases their awareness of the situation and problems of students.

37

A very important phenomenon has been the shift of the centre of gravity of INSET from exclusively shaping the personality and professional characteristics of the teacher to developing the educational staff and the institution where they teach in order to fulfil the demands arising from the socio-economic and cultural development.

The *basic structure* of INSET corresponds to the structure of pre-service training: it has its general, its academic subject and its pedagogical (professional) components, as well as its theoretical aspects. However, this does not mean that this structure, which is valid for INSET in general, has to be reproduced in all programmes. Of great significance is the fact that, from the viewpoint of the content of INSET, it is not specified in a syllabus. This means that, in principle, anything concerning human knowledge or activities can be taken up by the teacher as a self-educational task. In fact, however, the determination of subjects corresponds mainly to the needs of the educational system within which teachers work.

The following three needs stand out:

(a) the evaluation of the educational significance of new scientific knowledge, discoveries, new forms of art, new phenomena in the life of youth and society;
(b) the conduct and evaluation of educational experiments (production of new curriculum materials, educational technology, teaching methods etc.);
(c) the dissemination of innovations concerning the content, methods and organisation of education, i.e. the dissemination of changes generally considered as useful and feasible, such as new curricula or new educational technology.

In the course of its development the content of INSET has experienced different priorities and preferences. For example, with the growing threat of nuclear confrontation the issues of education for international understanding, co-operation and peace, and education related to human rights, fundamental freedoms and rights of nations have been paid greater attention; with the threat of ecological catastrophes the issues of environmental education have been introduced; with the arrival of computer technology in the classroom the issues of information technology in education have been initiated; the struggle against disease, drug abuse, alcohol, and AIDS has brought about the issues of health education; the necessity to evaluate in a critical way the information disseminated by mass media has justified media education etc.

As regards the *basic models* of INSET, the great variety of such models complicates their description and classification. In principle, however, two types of models can be found.

The first group includes the organisation-oriented models, in which the initiative is taken by the educational institution and/or the school administration at various levels. It provides a mechanism for identifying teacher potential and stimulating teachers to undergo purposeful professional growth.

The second group comprises the models based on the example of teachers who are expected to take the initiative for their own self-education. These models assume that the educational institution and/or school administration at the appropriate level will make resources available for the self-education of teachers, provided that teachers will take advantage of them.

Experience acquired so far seems to show that there is an opportunity to combine elements from both sorts of models in the realisation of INSET systems.

Models of INSET can be described in various ways. Mostly they are characterised by administrative or organisational procedures or measures, particularly in relation to procedures connected with the preparation of the curricula for INSET programmes and courses. The following specific features may be taken into account: the degree of centralisation within the system, the extent to which educational institutions have autonomy within this system and the status of teachers in these institutions. Where procedures are concerned, attention is focused mainly on the decision-making process concerning INSET, the identification of the need for INSET and the means for the integration of the results of INSET into the educational process. The procedures used in the preparation of curricula for INSET courses comprise first of all the training methods and the planning and development of the programmes.

INSET models are as varied as the socio-economic systems in which they operate. Thus, for example, education in the socialist countries, as a uniform and democratic system, incorporates INSET as an integral part. INSET is supervised and co-ordinated by a single entity. All teachers are involved and their lifelong education is viewed as a follow-up to their pre-service training. In the individual countries institutional bases have been set up for INSET and supervised by educational bodies at various levels. As well as the institutions actually carrying out INSET courses, teacher training colleges and teacher associations also participate in this process.

In the majority of countries the INSET system is not fully integrated into the educational system, even if, in view of the historical socio-economic and other origins of individual countries, many types of INSET exist. Nevertheless, there are efforts in evidence on the part of educational authorities aimed at achieving their rational interrelation according to an integrated national policy.

From the viewpoint of content, the vast majority of INSET courses contain elements of general education and culture, including political aspects, educational psychology and specialised professional components, together with the study of individual subjects.

2.3 Criticism of INSET provision

Currently, a number of criticisms are being levelled at particular aspects of INSET. For example, we often come across the fact that the objectives and the target groups of INSET are not clearly defined and sometimes even those who are involved in INSET are not aware of them. As mentioned above, at present we are witnessing significant efforts aimed at the clarification of the objectives of INSET and the orienting of INSET programmes to raising the standard of the teaching profession and, consequently, the quality of the educational process. There exist numerous examples of extensive INSET programmes where major parts are not relevant enough for those who participate in them. Sometimes we can also notice a certain obscurity with regard to the profile of qualifications required by the teacher as well as his or her mission in a progressively developing society.

An improvement is required in the procedures connected with approving the forms and content of INSET programmes, particularly where adequate consultation with teachers and their representatives is concerned. Other criticisms concern the failure to satisfy the demand for programmes on specific topics, the small variety of programmes in comparison with the spread of knowledge and experience among teachers, the selection procedures for participants in INSET courses, the insufficient evaluation of INSET activities, the relationship between INSET and functional and financial rewards for teachers and the lack of differentiation between teachers following different types of training (i.e. those involved in self-education; those participating in a course; those conducting research etc.).

Deficiencies are also reported in the administration, organisation and planning of INSET courses and in defining the objectives of individual forms and types of INSET. While insufficient attention has been paid to factors which limit the availability of resources, a better balance between the individual components of INSET is also required.

Efforts aimed at the improvement of INSET systems have run into a number of obstacles. These particularly concern innovatory programmes that are delayed by financial restrictions; teacher surplus and unemployment in some countries; the minimal financial means made available for INSET, especially for its more demanding and costly forms; insufficient moral and material incentives for teachers participating in courses, leading to a lack of willingness to participate and even a certain distrust of the actual effectiveness of INSET; scepticism concerning the ability of the ever more-qualified teacher to improve social relations and, last but not least, criticism of the quality and effectiveness of the forms of INSET made available to teachers.

Despite these criticisms, INSET has promoted their ability to differentiate, to maintain the internal dynamic of their profession, to improve the quality of the educational system, to assume proper attitudes and to increase the standard of the teaching and learning process in the light of educational reform and innovations.

3. ANTICIPATED FUTURE DEVELOPMENTS IN INSET

This brief assessment of the stage achieved in INSET and the trends manifested in this field on the basis of the above-mentioned analyses show that the time is ripe to deepen the concepts of INSET in the context of lifelong education in the nineties, especially on the basis of intensified INSET research.

3.1 Institutional and staff development
Let us recall the period ten years ago when selected European experts discussed in Prague (1977) information and research priorities in the field of INSET in the European region for the period at the beginning of the eighties. Could we at that time foresee the developments in INSET we are all familiar with now? Certainly not, and as a result we have not quite estimated the shift of the centre of gravity of INSET from shaping the personality and professional characteristics of the teacher to the development of the whole educational staff and the particular institution where they teach.

3.2 Needs of society
If INSET is oriented towards the development of the institution, which is to fulfil the demands arising from the socio-economic and cultural development of the society, it will also mean that in the nineties the centre of gravity of the in-service training of teachers will shift in favour of the needs of society, especially of the world of work. Within this context we are asking: what are

the social, economic, cultural and, last but not least, professional "imperatives" manifested at the end of the eighties and affecting the field of INSET? What else apart from the present state of INSET and its current trends could influence the evolution in this field in the nineties?

First of all, there are completely new ideas regarding educational systems which correspond to the needs of further socio-economic and cultural development at the turn of the millenium. Let us mention a few examples of such ideas.

3.3 Education and the world of work
Much has already been said about the relationship of the educational system to the world of work (see, for example, Gevers, 1987). If this relationship is to be efficient, closer interaction must inevitably develop between formal education and the system which is at present predominantly called adult education, and possibly their full integration into one progressive educational system.

This will bring about a significant change in both normal education and adult education in the context of a rational concept of lifelong education. This progressive system of lifelong education should be characterised by a close interaction with the world of work, if it aims to be efficient. This will have far-reaching consequences for the INSET system, stemming, *inter alia*, from the need for adequate interaction between the educational system and the world of work.

Thus, for instance, it will be necessary to fully respect the fact that the world of work and education are interdependent and inter-influential. The development of science and technology will most probably result in the disappearance of a still visible dividing line between the educational process as it is carried out at school and the further education process developing within social practice. The interaction between the educational system and the world of work will be well-founded through their mutual dialogue. We shall have to get used to the fact that the educational process is to an ever-increasing extent interrelated with practical activity. Periods of formal education will alternate with periods of social practice. The right to education and the duty to educate will not relate only to completing a certain number of grades of the educational system: it will have a lifelong effect.

3.4 Changing role of the teacher
A number of changing concepts of INSET are connected with the changing role of the teacher. Of great importance are considerations of the needs of INSET for the functions in the educational system which teachers will perform apart

from their specialisation and which will influence the structure of the teaching staff. These staffs will not only be teams of teachers of a certain specialisation. There will be a teacher with an additional function as counsellor, a teacher responsible for research and development, a teacher for the development of educational technology, a teacher for the application of information technology, a teacher for the development of simulation methods and educational-psychological games, a teacher for environmental education, a teacher specialised in international education, in media education, health education etc.

3.5 Rapid development of science and technology

The fact that science and technology will further dynamically develop is another factor influencing both the organisation and the content of INSET. There has always been some uncertainty concerning our knowledge of this development. However, some features have started to appear already, and will manifest themselves in the near future.

3.6 New teaching methods

Let us mention, for instance, teaching methods. They still bear the imprint of the methods applied in the course of centuries or even millenia — discussions with students, self-study, the reading and annotation of books. We are moving away from dictating and memorising. The introduction of new technology, especially micro-electronics and communication technology in education, leaves us in no doubt that the existing methods will fundamentally change.

We await further developments in the concept of computer-aided instruction and the use of interactive video. The broader and more efficient use of this new technology will influence not only the teaching and learning process but also the structure of education costs; most probably it will also have a social impact. However, what is really substantial in this respect is the fact that the role of the teacher will significantly change. First of all, classroom instruction will become a decreasing part of the teacher's activity in favour of activities based on the use of educational technology. This trend will result in the above-mentioned restructuring of education costs (the need for specialists, INSET in the application of new educational methods, investment in educational technology and the development of educational materials).

On the other hand, it is apparent that the methodological quality of teaching will be strongly enhanced and become more readily available to everybody. The teaching profession will be intellectually more demanding; it will be less monotonous and more diversified. The teacher will have more room for self-development and research and the exchange of experience with the world of work and social practice.

3.7 Impact of new methods on society

Changes in the teaching profession arising from radical shifts in educational methods have already been largely discussed. Less has been said about their impact on society. For instance, these new educational methods will contribute to an increase in the professional qualifications of an increasing number of working people. At the same time they will become familiar with new theoretical knowledge and experience. The systematic mastering of new educational methods and their adequate dissemination is a prerequisite for the realisation of a top quality and effective system of lifelong education of teachers and working people as a whole.

However, success will be achieved only when we are able to realise in formal education what has been proclaimed many times already: radically changing the system in order to enable it to teach young people how to learn, how to work with information, in other words to introduce them to a system of lifelong education. There is no doubting the range of implications this has for changes in the INSET system.

3.8 Greater inter-penetration between school and the outside world

Considerable implications for INSET will arise from the fact that the educational system will provide ever more relevant services for the world of work and vice-versa. Teachers from schools will be to an increasing extent involved in various programmes organised by enterprises, factories etc.and vice-versa. Schools will to a growing extent involve practising specialists in the educational process. Teachers will more often undergo periods in industry, offices and business in order to become familiar with innovations in social practice, and specialists from industry and business will be invited to schools to become acquainted with the latest theoretical achievements. Some experts speak about the process of deformalising the educational system and intensifying educational activity in social practice. In any case we shall move away from the traditional classroom and from the conception of the school as an encapsulated educational institution. The system of open education, distance learning, the system of a more refined social practice and the all-round use of education technology in all forms of educational activity will be further developed and expanded. Characteristics for further development will include a greater recognition of the importance of the verification of theoretical knowledge in practice and the gaining of practical experience,which will become a permanent component of formal education.

The educational system and the world of work are two different systems which must purposefully co-operate for the further development of society. The lack of such co-operation will inevitably result in the decrease of the efficiency of both, and will consequently hinder the development of society, the economy and culture.

3.9 New forms of evaluation
INSET in the nineties will also be affected by the development of methods for evaluating different types of INSET according to the demanding criteria of efficiency. In this connection numerous trends will be observed, such as the effort to increase the effectiveness of INSET by its adequate integration into a system which combines two other important aspects of lifelong education: the pre-service education of teachers and the daily experience of their working lives. It is expected that through pre-service training the teachers will acquire suitable techniques for their continuing self-education.

3.10 Incentives
Greater attention will be devoted to the creation and improvement of a system of incentives in order to make INSET an integral component of the professional life of teachers.

3.11 Teacher trainers
More systematic preparation and training will be devoted to those teachers involved in the pre-service and in-service training of teachers.

3.12 More teacher participation
Efforts will continue to be made to involve teachers in the decision-making process as it concerns the organisation of INSET programmes. Participation in decision-making will be more strongly related to school-based and school-focused, rather than teacher-focused, INSET courses.

3.13 More innovation in INSET and new themes
The trend toward trying out innovatory methods of INSET will be of increasing importance. This choice reflects such new problems confronting educational systems and society as environmental education, health education, international education, education and information technology, media education and education about the so-called global issues.

3.14 Longer INSET periods

The trend towards increasing the duration of INSET, particularly in regard to the period set aside for the practical application of theoretical knowledge, will continue.

3.15 Need for more international co-operation

Finally, let me mention a very important aspect which we have to take into account in our attempts to improve the standard of education. It is the need for more efficient international and regional co-operation in INSET and in education. Efficient international co-operation will have a positive impact not only on the quality of education but also on its cost structure. Moreover, it will contribute to promoting international co-operation and understanding in general, thereby strengthening peace and facilitating the joint solution of the global issues affecting the development of mankind.

4. CONCLUSION

This conference will present ideas on the development of the educational system in the years to come which will deeply influence INSET as early as the nineties. The above-mentioned examples should help us to consider and prepare for future trends and changes which have already started to emerge.

LITERATURE

1. *University Teaching and the Training of Teachers.* Proceedings of the European Regional Seminar organised by UNESCO in Prague, 25-29 November, 1985. Bucharest, European Centre for Higher Education, 1987, 87 p.
2. TMEJ, K. International Conference "Present Basic and Current Problems of In-service Teacher Education" (Ho-Chi-Min, VSR, November 1985). Newsletter EIC-FET Prague, 9, 1985, No. 2, pp 26-28.
3. HOPKINS, D. (Ed.) *In-service training and educational development.* An international survey. London, Croom Helm, 1986, 334 p.
4. HOEBEN, W. (Ed.) *In-service education of educational personnel in comparative perspective.* Report of a UNESCO joint study in the field of education. s -Gravenhage, Stichting voor Onderzoek van het Onderwijs, 1986. 220 s. Selecta reeks. Bibl. pp 207-218. Summary in English, French and Russian.
5. *Tomorrow's Teachers.* East Lansing, The Holmes Group Inc., 1986. 11, 96 p.

6. BLACKBURN, V. & MOISAN, C. *The in-service training of teachers in the twelve member states of the European Community.* Study carried out on behalf of the Commission of the European Communities, under the auspices of Le laboratoire de pédagogie expérimentale de l'Université de Liège. Maastricht, Presses Universitaires Européennes Maastricht, 1987. 63 p.

7. *New challenges for teachers and their education. National reports on teacher education.* Standing Conference of European Ministers of Education. 15th session. Strasbourg: Council of Europe, 1986. 156 p.

   Standing Conference of European Ministers of Education. 15th session, Helsinki 5-7 May 1987. *New challenges for teachers and their education. National reports on teacher education.* With an introduction on "Challenges met: trends in teacher education 1975-85" by Guy Neave. Diagrams on national teacher education systems by Hermann Neumeister. Strasbourg, Council of Europe 1987. 216. 25 p.

8. YFF, J. (Ed.) *The redesign of teacher education for the twenty-first century. International perspectives on the preparation of educational personnel.* Selected papers from the 30th Anniversary World Assembly, Washington DC, USA, 11-15 July 1983. Washington: the International Council on Education for Teaching, 1983. 134 p.

   YFF, J. (Ed.) Innovations in teacher education: the pursuit of excellence. *International Yearbook on Teacher Education 1984.* Selected papers from the Thirty-first World Assembly, Bangkok, Thailand, 23-27 July 1984. Washington DC: UNESCO 1984. 181 p.

   YFF, J. (Ed.) *Education in the Information Age: the Impact on Teacher Education 1985.* Selected papers from the Thirty-Second World Assembly, Vancouver, British Columbia, Canada, July 1985. Washington DC, 1985. 161 p.

9. VONK, J. H. C. & YREEDE, E. de, (Eds.) *In-service Education and Training of Teachers.* Lehrerfort- und Lehrerweiterbildung. Recyclage et formation continue des enseignants. Contributions to the Xth ATEE-Congress in Tilburg, Netherlands, 2-9 September 1985. Bruxelles/Amsterdam, ATEE, 1986. 267 p.

10. Teacher Education in the '80s and '90s. 4th International Seminar for Teacher Education. Seminar papers. Birmingham, 1984. Nestr.

    Teacher Education in the '80s and '90s. 5th International Seminar for Teacher Education. Seminar papers. Hosted by the University of Aveiro and the College of Education, Leiria, Portugal. Aveiro, 1985. Nestr.

    6th International Seminar for Teacher Education in the '80s and '90s, 13-19 June 1986, University of Regina, Saskatchevan, Canada. Seminar proceedings. University of Regina, 1986. 81 p.

11. ISSED — International Seminar on Staff and Educational Development. Newcastle 1984; Leysin, 1985; Witzenhausen, 1986; Newcastle, 1987.

12. GEVERS, J. K. M. The keynote address. Teacher education and the world of work. New economic, social and professional imperatives for the twenty-first century. ICET World Assembly. Eindhoven, the Netherlands, 20-24 July 1987. The Hague: ICET, 1987. 16 p.

13. PETRÁČEK, S. *Trends in in-service education.* Prague, EIC-FET, 1985. 61 p.

BIBLIOGRAPHY

1. European Information Centre of Charles University for the Further Education of Teachers. *Further education of teachers. Selected annotated bibliography*, Vol. 1 (1970-76). Prague, 1978, 257 p.
2. European Information Centre of Charles University for the Further Education of Teachers. *Further education of teachers. Selected annotated bibliography*, Vol. 2 (1977-78). Prague, 1980, 328 p.
3. European Information Centre of Charles University for the Further Education of Teachers. *Further education of teachers. Selected annotated bibliography*, Vol. 3 (1979-80). Prague, 1982, 328 p.
4. European Information Centre of Charles University for the Further Education of Teachers. *Further education of teachers. Selected annotated bibliography*, Vol. 4 (1981-88). Prague, 1988.
5. Charles University, Czechoslovakia. European Information Centre for the Further Education of Teachers. "In-service teacher education". *Educational documentation and information* (Paris: Geneva, UNESCO: IBE), Nos. 218/219, 1st/2nd quarter 1981. 99 p.
6. Charles University, Czechoslovakia. European Information Centre for the Further Education of Teachers. "In-service teacher education". *Bulletin of the International Bureau of Education* (Paris: Geneva, UNESCO: IBE), 234/235, 1st/2nd quarter 1985. 214 p.

3
Review of Research on In-Service Education: a U.K. Perspective

Michael Eraut
United Kingdom

SUMMARY

The paper presents a typology of INSET based on three main types of knowledge — Subject Matter Knowledge, Educational Knowledge and Societal Knowledge — and five modes of knowledge use — classroom, classroom-related, management, other professional and purely personal. It argues that INSET should be defined to cover all activities whose purpose is to promote the learning of teachers, not just those which are included in formally organised courses. Even with courses the link between off-the-job and on-the-job learning is critical, especially for classroom or classroom-related modes of use.

The review then focuses on three issues now perceived as fundamental. First, approaches to needs assessment are examined: these include centrally determined needs, and decentralised approaches such as teacher self-evaluation, supervision and appraisal, school self-review and inspection. Second, research into teachers' practical knowledge is examined with particular attention to how it is learned and how it is used. Third, there is a brief discussion of factors affecting the success of INSET, a topic which has been rather more fully researched.

Throughout the paper it is argued that more fundamental research into INSET is needed than has hitherto been common. Course evaluation alone is insufficiently penetrating to provide much guidance for future policy. The prime purpose of the paper is to indicate some directions in which research of both theoretical and practical value might usefully proceed.

1. MAPPING THE DOMAIN

This paper does not seek to elaborate upon or justify the various functions and purposes of INSET; but it is nevertheless useful to start with a map of the domain. The first dimension in Figure 1 simply distinguishes between three types of Knowledge. Subject Knowledge comprises that knowledge which is found in school syllabuses and which is formally taught to pupils. Education Knowledge includes all that knowledge, both theoretical and practical, which impinges upon the teaching process in particular and educational provision in general. Societal Knowledge incorporates both that experiential and common-sense knowledge which is acquired by living in a society, and that more organised and focused knowledge of society which might be deemed important for good citizenship. Clearly there are areas of overlap between these three categories and they are all capable of being subdivided in a number of ways.

Figure 1

		Types of Knowledge		
		Subject Matter Knowledge	Educational Knowledge	Societal Knowledge
Mode of Use	Classroom			
	Classroom Related			
	Management			
	Other Professional			
	Purely Personal			

The second dimension indicates how this knowledge is likely to be used. Classroom knowledge is built into the actual process of teaching and incorporates much of what is sometimes described as 'practical know-how': much of it is learned on-the-job, and it is difficult to codify and describe. Classroom-related Knowledge, on the other hand, is more easily described than applied. Such knowledge has to be interpreted, transformed and integrated with classroom knowledge before it can be said to be genuinely in use. The potential range of such knowledge is very large, and there is considerable professional dispute about which aspects are most important. Management Knowledge is important for senior teachers, principals, supervisors, inspectors and administrators. Like knowledge of teaching it can be subdivided into job-embedded and job-related categories (cf. Howey and Joyce, 1978). Other Professional Knowledge covers such areas as curriculum development, pupil counselling and communication with parents, which contribute to the life of the school and indeed to the profession in general. It manifests itself through non-teaching roles within the schools and through participation in innovative activities, committees, working parties, development of learning resources etc. Sometimes the acquisition of such knowledge is viewed largely in terms of career development, either because it forms part of some formal qualification or because it is hoped that it will improve the chance of being promoted.

Returning to the first dimension, the area of Societal Knowledge is probably that which is most neglected. Although teachers are members of the society in which they work, they tend to be more familiar with some aspects and sub-cultures than with others. Their relative isolation from some groups and activities can limit their vision, their understanding and their capacity to prepare young people for the future. There is even the recognised phenomena of teachers 'who have never left school'. Evidence of this emerges from research studies whose primary foci are elsewhere; and the issue is often discussed. But no direct research has ensued. We now have INSET programmes to give teachers the opportunity of gaining experience working in industry, but not for them to experience other occupations or live in other cultural settings. Perhaps this is a sign of the times. Even these programmes, however, have been only minimally evaluated.

INSET aimed at improving Subject Matter Knowledge is much more common, though much of it bypasses the formal INSET system by being included in general provision for adult education, for which teacher participation statistics do not even exist. Similarly, non-formal education through television, newspapers and local societies plays an important part in some teachers' continuing

51

education. Formal programmes tend to be categorised as supplementary (a euphemism for remedying deficiencies in initial training) conversion or updating.

There has been very little evaluation of such courses; but there is evidence from other sources, including research into initial training, to suggest that many of them are not ideally conceived for their purpose. One problem is a growing recognition among cognitive psychologists and researchers into subject curricula and pedagogy that knowledge of a subject is much more complex than had been assumed previously. Some of the conceptual frameworks and methods of inquiry are acquired semi-consciously by a process of socialisation into the culture of the discipline, and may not be explicitly taught in a manner which enables them to be easily communicated to others. At the same time people have become more aware of the need for students to consciously develop their own conceptual frameworks. So learning a subject to a certain level in higher education does not prepare a teacher for structuring, sequencing and pacing their lessons; for communicating the ideas to pupils who may be less intelligent and younger than themselves; for recognising the potential in pupils' questions; or for understanding the nature of pupil misconceptions. To become proficient in these aspects of subject teaching, teachers have to reorganise and rework their knowledge into forms appropriate for classroom use. Their subject matter knowledge remains job-related rather than job-embedded unless and until this further learning has occurred.

The bulk of this paper, however, is concerned with Educational Knowledge, particularly that which falls within the classroom and classroom-related categories. Central to nearly all planning of INSET in these categories are the assumptions (1) that teachers' knowledge and skills will be enhanced (2) that teachers' attitudes and classroom behaviour will change and (3) that pupils will ultimately benefit. Thus the effectiveness of INSET is crucially dependent on teachers' learning: first in the INSET context; and secondly, and even more importantly in their own classrooms. From this it follows that research into INSET has to take into account all occasions and situations where teacher learning occurs. INSET must be defined not simply in terms of courses but to cover ''all those activities whose purpose is to enhance, promote or support the learning of serving teachers''. This definition includes activities which are commonly discussed under such headings as supervision, staff development and curriculum implementation. Indeed many INSET strategies now involve combinations of course-based and non course-based activities.

Research into INSET should derive considerable benefit in the future from expanding its boundaries in this way, not only by linking with research in cognate areas like curriculum implementation but also by importing ideas from the wider domain of adult education and training and more specifically from other types of continuing professional education. Meanwhile progress is seriously impeded by a fixation on courses, because that is how INSET is administratively defined. Recent British experience is summarised by Bolam (1988) who characterised good courses as having the following features:

— collaborative planning involving course leaders, LEA sponsors and former or prospective participants;
— a clear focus upon participants' current and future needs;
— careful preparatory briefing for participants several weeks ahead of the course, with opportunities for pre-course work where appropriate;
— a programme which is structured but has enough flexibility to allow for modifications in the light of monitoring and formative evaluation;
— a programme which is oriented towards experience, practice and action, and using, as appropriate, methods like action learning, action research, performance feedback and on-the-job assistance;
— a 'sandwich' timetable including course-based and job-based experiences to facilitate this approach;
— careful de-briefing after the course and sustained support, ideally including on-the-job assistance where new skills are being implemented.

These conclusions are supported by evidence from both research projects (Bailey, 1987; Ruddock, 1981) and course evaluations (Wallace, 1988); and they also correspond quite closely with a list of INSET weaknesses derived by Fullan (1982) from the North American literature — Bolam's positive points being opposite versions of Fullan's weaknesses. An important feature of this list is that five of the seven recommendations contain some reference to off-course events or activities. Clearly the concept of INSET as courses is here being stretched to the very limit. Indeed Bolam himself goes beyond it to consider school-focused INSET and staff development.

However, it is not just broadening the scope of INSET that is needed but deepening as well. Fullan (1982) argued that "there is a profound lack of any conceptual basis in the planning and implementing of in-service programmes that would ensure their effectiveness." Rules of thumb derived from numerous course evaluations and the collective wisdom of experienced professionals can no longer substitute for penetrating research which seeks to address more fundamental questions. The distinguished members of this conference will no doubt compile a formidable agenda of such questions, but for the present I have to use my own.

(1) How are INSET needs identified, articulated, communicated and prioritised by various groups?
(2) What kind of knowledge is learned during INSET and how is it learned?
(3) How is such knowledge derived from, related to, or embedded in ongoing practice?
(4) What factors facilitate or inhibit these processes?

2. NEEDS ASSESSMENT

To suggest, as do most writers on INSET, that INSET planning should be based on assessment of need is to pose questions rather than to provide answers. Whose needs are to be assessed? Those of a particular group of pupils, an individual teacher, a department within a school, the school itself, the district, or even the nation? And who will be making the assessment? One clear finding of research is that if INSET participants do not recognise a need as having sufficient priority for them, activities aimed at meeting that need will be judged irrelevant. Yet it would be undemocratic if teachers were to be regarded as the sole definers of INSET needs without considering the views of other members of society. This suggests two possible strategies for INSET managers:

> either considerable effort is devoted before or during INSET to convincing participants of the importance of certain needs
> or the needs assessment process is decentralised so that schools and teachers define their own needs, with some safeguard to ensure that the views of other groups are taken into account.

The 1986 reform of INSET in England and Wales resulted in a clearly formulated combination of these strategies, within a scheme where central government funded a proportion of local INSET costs up to an agreed ceiling and after approval of a proposed local programme. This programme is divided between national priorities, such as Science Education or School Management, and local priorities. Significantly, local districts are required to evaluate their programmes and to justify their assessment of local needs with evidence of teacher consultation. Many local districts have effectively delegated a proportion of these funds for individual schools to spend according to their own internal assessment of need, subject only to approval by the district authority. Neither of the strategies outlined above is totally new, so there is some evidence of how they work.

The determination of national priorities for educational change is the domain of educational policy research, into which I do not propose to intrude. But the translation of such policy into statements of INSET needs and the acknowledgement by teachers of these needs are central to our concern for effective INSET. Let me cite three examples, each of which would benefit from more detailed research.

2.1 The Introduction of GCSE
This summer, the majority of English and Welsh 16 year olds took a new national examination, the General Certificate of Secondary Education (GCSE). This differed from its predecessors in many significant ways, both in the kinds of knowledge being assessed and in the methods of assessment. Although some change of this type had long been advanced by many teachers, the decision to introduce the new examination came quite suddenly and the detailed requirements in individual subjects were spelt out in syllabus form at very short notice. Hence the change was regarded by teachers as externally imposed. Nevertheless, it was unavoidable; and preparation for GCSE was immediately recognised by all concerned as the major priority for INSET, even to the extent of swamping most other thinking about the INSET needs of secondary schools. Any INSET of quality which addressed these needs was bound to be successful. The fact that much of it was not so regarded is an indictment of the way it was managed and planned, confirming that knowledge about effective INSET has not been well   disseminated, especially to policy makers (Radnor, 1987).

2.2 School Relations with Industry and Commerce
For at least 10 years the British government has been advocating that pupils and teachers should have greater knowledge of the "world of work", particularly of industry and commerce. The innovation strategy has been one of persuasion and financial incentives for change. Persuasion has included government reports and comments by Her Majesty's Inspectors, politicians and industrialists; and it undoubtedly received an enormous boost from universal concern about growing youth unemployment in the early 1980s. Financial incentives have been dominated by the Technical and Vocational Education Initiative (TVEI), in which the Manpower Services Commission provided a selected number of schools with enhanced facilities, equipment and staffing; but there have also been several specially financed INSET programmes. Only one of these INSET programmes, the influential TRIST (TVEI Related In-Service Training) pro-

gramme which ran from 1985-7 and in some areas acted as a pilot for the new national INSET policy, was properly evaluated. There is good evidence that this long-term innovation strategy has succeeded in changing attitudes and developing new policies in most schools. The major constraints now come from conflicts with other government policies, notably the traditional academic bias still found in GCSE, university entrance examinations (A Levels) and judging schools in terms of their success with able pupils alone. The evaluations of TRIST, however, have shown up many weaknesses in the way that INSET programmes have traditionally been planned and delivered, as well as drawing attention to some innovative strategies that have been extremely successful (Holly et al., 1987; Oldroyd and Hall, 1988; Eraut et al., 1988).

2.3 School-Parent Relations

Relations between schools and parents have also been a major government concern for at least twenty years. Government publications and reports, and parent organisations have kept the issue in a fairly prominent position throughout this period; and it has even been reflected in legislation. However, there has been little financial support for programmes outside poor or multicultural communities, and only some of these programmes have had a strong parent dimension. At no time have school-parent relations been identified as a major INSET need for all schools. In my view this has been a mistake (cf. Becher et al., 1979), so why has it not happened? One possible explanation is that it is thought to be teacher attitudes which need changing, not knowledge and skills, thus revealing a failure to recognise the potential of more experiential types of INSET for affecting changes in attitude. Another explanation is that, unlike the two examples above, the argument for changes in school-parent relations is based not on responding to new needs but on current practice being branded as deficient. Schools and teachers felt they were being criticised in a potentially vulnerable area; and their natural reaction was not to take ownership of the problem but to transfer the blame.

These and other examples have revealed that there are two levels of needs assessment, the policy level and the planning level. The first informs the decision to mount an INSET programme in a particular area for a particular group of clients; while the second informs the more detailed planning of INSET activities to meet the more specific needs of these clients. The evidence from the above examples is that many INSET planners and providers lack the knowledge to translate policy into well-designed INSET programmes; and that in some cases, notably GCSE, they are given an impossible brief because policy-makers fail to recognise the order of magnitude of the task. A further weakness endemic in centralised systems of provision is bad preparation and management. Teachers find themselves on courses at very short notice with little idea of why they were selected or what they will be expected to do on their return. When teachers of varying knowledge, experience and attitudes arrive on a course without any clear brief from their schools the task of the INSET provider is virtually impossible. This is still common practice, but it may diminish in frequency as schools take more responsibility for their own needs assessments.

So let us now return to the second, decentralised, needs assessment strategy. The diagram below shows four possible forms this may take.

INITIATOR \ LEVEL	Internal	External
Individual Teacher	Teacher Self-evaluation	Supervision Appraisal
School or Department	School Self-review	Inspection

The literature on supervision gives relatively little attention to outcomes, being more concerned with the training of supervisors than with evidence on how supervision affects the quality of teaching. The main issues discussed are the diagnosis of teacher needs and the supervisor-supervisee relationship. But there are few independent accounts of the intervention process and little attention is given to the nature of the learning opportunities provided for teachers. A simple research agenda would be to ask:

— on what basis does a supervisor diagnose a teacher's needs?
— how reliable or valid is a supervisor's judgement?
— to what extent is the diagnosis agreed or shared?
— what actions follow?
— to what extent do these actions achieve their intended purpose?

In Britain most supervision is within the school by a headteacher or head of department. This has usually taken the form of relatively unobtrusive monitoring, with senior teachers only intervening in situations considered to be serious, thus maintaining the norm of teacher autonomy or what Lortie (1975) described as the distinctive zones of influence of principal and teacher. However, Britain is about to introduce a system of teacher appraisal, which requires regular (possibly annual) reviews of each teacher's performance. This will result, I predict, in INSET resources being directed towards needs identified in this way. Otherwise the whole exercise will be discredited. But there will also be a tendency for appraiser and apraisee to collude in reporting successful progress. So independent research into the quality of the diagnosis, the quality of subsequent learning opportunities and their effect on subsequent teaching performance, will be vital.

There is even less research information available on school inspection and its subsequent effects on those inspected. Given the important role of both national and local inspectors in Britain this is a very serious omission. In the case of inspection there is a particularly large gap between a report on a school and any subsequent identification of INSET needs. Part of the problem is probably a traditional fixation on course-based modes of INSET. Other learning opportunities like visits or coaching do not even get considered.

School self-review has been gaining impetus in Britain for about ten years. Sometimes Local Education Authorities (LEAs) have required schools to do it, often within a prescribed format; sometimes they have only recommended it; sometimes schools themselves have taken the initiative. Reasons given have included external accountability, improved internal management, and more recently the identification of needs. There is evidence to show that, if taken seriously, the review process is extremely time-consuming. But do the benefits justify the costs? So far the evidence for externally imposed self-review has not been encouraging (Clift et al., 1987). Such reviews tend to avoid revealing internal weaknesses and concentrate on deficiencies in resourcing. The effect of internal initiatives is difficult to judge because they are so rarely evaluated or even publicly reported. When information does become available it is usually from the scheme's initiator or coordinator. Those of us with ears to the ground would probably agree that there have been many failures and some notable successes. My own view is that schools have been far too ambitious in trying to introduce all-embracing schemes when they have little prior experience to build on and few staff with any training in evaluation. It is these all-embracing schemes which have tended to dominate the literature and attracted the sponsorship of education agencies.

Several major weaknesses are readily apparent in the school self-review movement:

(1) often a review creates a temporary burst of enthusiasm and staff involvement, but this does not get translated into appropriate action. Hence the idea is rapidly discredited;
(2) there is no attempt in most cases to collect any new evidence, and this lack of evaluation knowledge shows. What is collected is a range of current opinions, and only some of those contributing opinions have given much time to prior thought or discussion;
(3) people tend to perceive their current situations in a conservative and relatively complacent way: they see what they want to see and report what they want to report;
(4) external and independent views are rarely included;
(5) the highly political nature of the process is often ignored;
(6) the psychological barriers to publicly admitting a need are also ignored;
(7) the process is highly dependent on the organisational climate, on the priority given it by teachers, on how teachers read 'the hidden agendas', on the nature of people's concerns about possible consequences.

Most schools do not yet know how best to manage, implement and follow-up school self-reviews; and until they do their potential will be hard to determine.

Asking a school to assess its needs for staff-development may not involve it in any kind of self-review, though many of the points made above will still be relevant (Hewton, 1987). What often occurs is a process better described as the negotiation of wants. The resulting proposal will usually contain genuine needs, but they might not be those to which an independent outsider would have given greatest priority. Two kinds of need are likely to dominate: new developments and career-related needs. The need for INSET is admissible when there is something new, and one's job is being redirected or redefined in some way; but not when there is something that simply needs to be improved, because that implies some deficiency. This raises a research question of crucial significance for the future of INSET: **under what conditions and circumstances will teachers diagnose their own learning needs, engage in the collection of evidence to deepen that diagnosis, or agree with a diagnosis made by another person?**

The major emphasis of the literature on teacher development and classroom action research has been on such teacher self-evaluation. The argument has been that needs are best identified by teachers researching into their own

59

classrooms. A growing number of British teachers have embraced this approach with some enthusiasm, often with support from higher education institutions. Elliott (1980), Day (1981) and Ashton et al. (1983) have provided rationales and procedures to guide such work; and there are many teacher networks providing mutual support. Large numbers of self-reports have been published, of varying degrees of utility to those seeking good evidence of success. However, the suspicion remains that only a small minority of teachers are prepared to undertake this kind of activity: the question about teacher self-diagnosis posed above remains only partially answered. Also needed is some research which takes an independent perspective on classroom action research, particularly with respect to possible positive outcomes for pupils.

Research into teacher diagnosis of needs will also need to look more deeply into issues of self-perception, situational perception, awareness of alternatives and institutional micropolitics. Eraut (1987) has analysed the basic logic of the needs assessment process as follows:

"Logically, to define a need for a child, teacher, department, school or even LEA implies

(a)   some view of the current situation; and
(b)   aspirations for, or expectations of, a future situation that is different.

The quality of needs assessment will depend on both these factors. For example, a person's view of the current situation will comprise

— information about context, conditions, processes, activities, intentions and outcomes
— standards, values and criteria by which these are judged
— frameworks and perspectives which determine how it is interpreted and understood.

All this may be either taken for granted or derived by a process of enquiry and reflection. Usually, there is a bit of both. Always there is scope for improvement by collecting more information, by reflecting more on values and by becoming more aware of other perspectives and interpretations.

In a similar way, thinking about the future must necessarily involve:

— some awareness of alternatives to current policy and practice
— some assessment of the feasibility of these options
— some evaluation of the desirability of options and their anticipated outcomes.

The second of these usually presents the greatest problem for British teachers and administrators, who tend to rapidly assess significant change as impractical. Needs then get defined in terms of marginal improvements in current practice or 'more of the same'. Thus an individual's assessment of need is limited both by their perception and understanding of their current situation and by their vision of possible alternatives to it.''

This analysis has three implications. First, it suggests fruitful lines of inquiry for research into needs assessment. Second, it shows how improving the quality of needs assessment could itself be a primary purpose for INSET. Third, it suggests an important role for school-based evaluation in gathering evidence both to guide diagnoses of current situations and to improve the analysis of possible options (Eraut 1984).

Returning to the question of school micropolitics and indeed of curriculum politics at district and national level, Eraut (1987) argues that:

> The inherent difficulty and the controversial nature of needs assessment become even more apparent when one takes seriously the notion of the pupil as the ultimate client. Any statement of teachers' needs or school needs is predicated on some view of what teachers should be doing for their pupils. It incorporates judgements about the curriculum, about teaching and about the purpose of schooling which are essential to any concept of quality in education.

Such judgments are often contested, sometimes in private and sometimes in public. Within schools, for example, many formal and informal discussions about policy and practice can be interpreted in terms of negotiations about needs assessment. Moreover, power and position often play as important a part in such discussions as evidence and reason. Research which neglected this political perspective would be missing an important dimension.

3. TEACHERS' EDUCATIONAL KNOWLEDGE: HOW IS IT LEARNED AND HOW IS IT USED?

It was suggested earlier that INSET often loses effectiveness because detailed planning fails to clarify sufficiently the knowledge and skills to be learned. Initial teacher training suffers from similar problems, and the two are not unrelated. The definition of what counts as educational knowledge has been heavily influenced by higher education institutions, which have a vested interest in emphasising the more theoretical aspects, because these have higher status in a higher education environment. Hence teacher education became increasingly theoretical during the 1960s and early 1970s, closely identifying itself with the social sciences. As theory became increasingly isolated from classroom practice, the relationship between education courses and practical teaching was unclear to many teachers. Even so-called "professional courses" tended to supply idealised models of teaching, which were consigned to storage when found to be unusable in practice. During the last decade, however, the balance has been considerably redressed (Alexander et al., 1984).

The result has been the growth of a new field of research, whose members have eschewed doing research on teaching in the traditional manner of the social sciences in favour of studying the knowledge and skills that teachers use in their classrooms. Teaching is perceived as too complex and too situation-specific to be studied by traditional research methods; and perhaps after all it is the good teachers who know best! Valuable accounts of research in this tradition can be found in Brown and McIntyre (1986), Calderhead (1988) and Clark (1986). The major difficulty found by this research is of great significance for INSET: most of teachers' practical classroom knowledge is intuitive, routinised and tacit. They cannot explain very much of what they know and do. Their practical knowledge is learned through experience without being explicitly formalised; and it is used intuitively more often than rationally. Moreover, teachers have to develop habits and routines in order to cope and survive in the classroom; but this results in their becoming wedded to forms of practice in a manner that inhibits subsequent change.

In spite of this routinisation of many aspects, teaching is so complex that teachers still have to think a great deal about it, both preactively (when preparing for teaching) and interactively (while still engaged in teaching). Research into teachers' thinking is beginning to elucidate the nature of some of this thought, but it also confirms that the unpredictability of teaching is a disincentive to too much forward planning. Classroom decision-making takes place very rapidly under conditions of extreme complexity and uncertainty. It is not cool and deliberate, but hot and hurried, not easily recalled for subsequent reflection. Thus it is not surprising, as Clark (1986) notes, that:

> "teachers develop and hold implicit theories about their students, about the subject matter that they teach and about their roles and responsibilities and how they should act. These implicit theories are not neat and complete reproductions of the educational psychology found in textbooks or lecture notes. Rather, teachers' implicit theories tend to be eclectic aggregations of cause-effect propositions from many sources, rules of thumb, generalizations drawn from

personal experience, beliefs, values, biases, and prejudices. Teachers are subject to the full range of insights and errors in human judgement (described by Nisbett and Ross, 1980), just as all humans are when faced with complex, real time, consequential, and occasionally emotion-laden social judgements and action situations.''

The overwhelming conclusion of all this research is that the prime source of a teacher's practical knowledge is their own classroom experience. At worst, they learn a set of almost unthinking routines, that become progressively dysfunctional over time. At best, they continue to learn and adapt by continually reflecting on their experience. From this perspective, teacher learning derives both from new experience or newly interpreted experience and from reflection on that experience. Thus new ideas about teaching will only become relevant if (a) teachers are persuaded and helped to try something new and persist through all the difficulties or (b) the ideas affect the way teachers interpret their current or previous experience. Well-designed INSET is capable of fulfilling these functions; but the effect will be only temporary, unless the full implications of teachers learning to change their classroom practice are understood and taken into account.

Eraut (1982) discusses how new knowledge introduced during INSET is likely to be used, and how the process is affected by the context and conditions of use. Most learning, he argues, takes place when a teacher tries to use a new idea and not when the idea was first introduced and discussed. Learning is like an iceberg. The introduction and early comprehension of an idea is explicit and visible, above the surface, but only a small proportion of the total. Most learning takes place during subsequent attempts to use the idea. Such learning is individual, private, invisible and below the surface. INSET often attends only to the easy part above the surface but neglects the difficult part below the surface when teachers struggle to put the idea into practice on their own.

Another implication of this use-oriented view of learning is that ideas learned in one context are difficult to transfer to another. Thus Eraut contrasts the three contexts of academic learning, school-wide discussion and classroom teaching, and suggests that ideas only transfer with difficulty from one to another. The most difficult of these contexts is the classroom itself, because incorporating new ideas into classroom practice involves a great deal of unlearning and the abandonment of routines that have enabled a teacher to cope with the stresses of daily classroom life. Changing one's teaching style involves deskilling, risk, information overload and mental strain, and in addition to practical help there is considerable need for psychological support (Day, 1981).

The reader may note that we now have the beginnings of a theoretical underpinning for Bolam's empirical conclusions; and his emphasis on job-based experience or assistance in three of his seven conclusions is more readily appreciated; so also is the magnitude of the task of helping a teacher change their classroom role, which, according to Stallings (1979), requires at least a year of classroombased support. By these standards much INSET provision has been only a token response to problems which require action of a quite different order of magnitude.

Let us now briefly examine some of the approaches which try to meet Bolam's conditions. The most clearly articulated from a theoretical viewpoint is probably the skill-training model of Joyce and Showers (1980). They distinguish between five principal training methods or components and argue that all five are necessary to achieve lasting impact in the classroom:

> "(1) presentation/description (e.g. via lecture/discussion) of new skills and underlying theory;
> (2) modelling the new skills (e.g. via live demonstration or video);
> (3) practising the new skills in simulated and controlled conditions (e.g. with peers or with small groups of children);
> (4) feedback on performance of new skills (e.g. using a structured system/instrument or unstructured discussion) in simulated and/or real settings;
> (5) teaching for application, transfer and integration via in-classroom and in-school assistance from peers and from trainers.''

This approach assumes a skill-based analysis of teacher knowledge and clearly derives from earlier research on microteaching. The main difference from the original microteaching format is the addition of a vital fifth step, which they describe as ''coaching''. Hitherto coaching had been rarely used after initial training, but Joyce and Showers have evidence that it significantly improves the transfer of learning from INSET to classroom settings (Showers, 1985).

Another approach increasingly used in the U.K. is the appointment of good classroom teachers as advisory teachers, whose duties may include working alongside teachers in their own classrooms and supporting school-based INSET. Although the general curriculum principles are part of their brief, their purpose is not to implement an externally specified innovation. They work in partnership with classroom teachers to evolve a model of practice which suits their clients while still meeting the general curricular aims they are employed to support. Some modelling may be done in the client's own classroom, and this is followed by joint teaching and a gradual transfer of responsibility from consultant to client. There is casestudy evidence to support the success of this strategy but there has been no systematic large-scale evaluation. There is also some evidence that an element of formal INSET can reduce the time needed by providing a group of 'clients' with a general understanding of central ideas, but cannot substitute for the individual classroom support.

A third approach, recently developed in Britain, is the multiphase INSET course interspersed with school-based activities. Very positivie evaluations have been made of courses which have been welldesigned according to this strategy. Some of the teacher selfevaluations designed earlier took place within a course format of this kind. Others have focussed more on the responsibilities of senior teachers for school-based evaluation and development, and some on specifically managerial roles. Important for the success of such courses are a thorough analysis of the knowledge and skills being developed, tutors with a commitment to interactive sessions which use the experience of the participants, the willing involvement of participants' schools and sufficient financial support. Not all the aims of such courses are concerned with the development of new skills; equally important are aims concerned with improving senior teacher's capacities to analyse school situations and assess pupil and teacher needs. A detailed discussion of the theoretical and practical aspects of this problem can be found in Eraut (1988).

4. FACTORS AFFECTING THE SUCCESS OF INSET

This section will be short as this territory has been thoroughly explored by the literature on curriculum implementation (Fullan, 1982; Huberman and Miles, 1984) and by recent reviews of INSET (Blackburn and Moisan, 1987; Bolam, 1988; Eraut, 1985; Petracek, 1986). It should be noted, however, that recent British research has confirmed the critical role played by principals and senior teachers in the internal management not only of INSET and staff development but also of the school climate and whether it supports or inhibits teacher learning. In particular:

(1) the pattern of rewards, including praise and promotion, will encourage or discourage classroom change;
(2) rhetorical exhortation usually increases teacher scepticism;
(3) school norms may inhibit attempts at change. In particular there is a tendency to focus more on pupil behaviour and coverage of the syllabus than on how much pupils actually learn;

(4) the school may not provide sufficient time for reflection or occasions when colleagues can share their experiences;

(5) the school may not give the teacher access to learning opportunities matched to their individual needs;

(6) the opportunity for classroom intervisiting is heavily dependent on administrative support;

(7) the timing of changes in curricula, textbooks, examinations etc. rarely dovetails with INSET opportunities; so that each is constrained by the absence of the other.

Eraut et al. (1988) argue that these school effects are so important that INSET initiatives which try to influence schools that have not yet developed the appropriate staff development climate and infrastructure are unlikely to succeed. More INSET resources, they suggest, should be devoted to training school managers to develop the appropriate conditions within their schools.

5. CONCLUSIONS

The field of in-service education has not been widely or deeply researched. Evaluations alone are insufficient because they rarely have the opportunity to address more fundamental issues. It seems to be universally agreed that effective INSET is vital for the future quality of education. So a more fundamental programme of research is urgently needed. This paper, therefore, has given considerable attention to outlining the kind of research that is needed.

The very practical issue of needs assessment has also been stressed, because this is consistently revealed as a weakness in INSET policy and practice. Unless there is agreement on needs, the preconditions for successful INSET are unlikely to be met.

Another research finding with policy implications is that effective INSET programmes tend to be fairly long and expensive. Planners often underestimate by an order of magnitude what is needed to achieve their goals. Therefore resources will have to be more concentrated and more clearly focused on priorities. Attempting to do too much and failing undermines teacher morale, supports conservatism and effectively inoculates teachers against responding favourably to future proposals for change.

LITERATURE

ALEXANDER, R., CRAFT, M. & LYNCH, J. (eds) (1984) *Change in Teacher Education, Context and Provision since Robbins.* Holt-Saunders.

ASHTON, P.M.E. et al. (1983) *Teacher Education in the Classroom: Initial and In-Service.* Croom Helm.

BAILEY, A.J. (1987) *Support for School Management.* Croom Helm.

BECHER, R.A., ERAUT, M.R. et al. (1979) *Accountability in the Middle Years of Schooling.* Project Report. University of Sussex Education Area.

BLACKBURN, V. & MOISAN, C. (1987) *The in-service training of teachers in the twelve Member States of the European Community.* Presses Inter-universitaires Europeennes Maastricht.

BOLAM, R. (1988) "What is Effective INSET?" *Professional Development and INSET.* Proceedings of the 1987 NFER Members Conference. National Foundation for Educational Research, Slough.

BROWN, S. & McINTYRE, D. (1986) *The Qualities of Teachers: Building on Professional Craft Knowledge.* Scottish Council for Research in Education.

CALDERHEAD, J. (ed) (1988) *Teachers' Professional Learning.* Falmer Press.

CLARK, C.M. (1986) "Asking the Right Questions about Teacher Preparation: Contributions of Research on Teacher Thinking". Paper presented to International Study Association on Teacher Thinking. Leuven, Belgium.

CLIFT, P.S., NUTTALL, D.L. & McCORMICK, R. (eds) (1987) *Studies in School Self-Evaluation.* Falmer Press.

DAY, C. (1981) *Classroom-Based In-Service Teacher Education: The Development and Evaluation of a Client-Centred Model.* Occasional Paper 9, University of Sussex Education Area.

ELLIOTT, J. (1980) 'Implications of classroom research for professional development' in Hoyle, E. & Megarry, J. (eds) *World Yearbook of Education 1980: Professional Development of Teachers.*

ERAUT, M. (1982) "What is Learned in In-Service Education and How? A knowledge Use Perspective". *British Journal of In-Service Education*, Vol. 9, No. 1. (French language version in Ducros, P. & Finkelsztein, D. (eds) *L'école face de changement.* Centre Régional de Documentation Pédagogique de l'Académie de Grenoble.)

ERAUT, M. (1985) "In-service Teacher Education" in Husen, T. & Postlethwaite, N. (eds) *International Encyclopedia of Education.* Pergamon Press.

ERAUT, M. (1987) "Evaluation and Quality Management". *Management in Education*, Vol. 1, No. 2.

ERAUT, M., PENNYCUICK, D. & RADNOR, H. (1988) *Local Evaluation of INSET: a meta-evaluation of TRIST Evaluations.* NDCSMT, University of Bristol School of Education.

ERAUT, M. (1988) "Learning about Management — the role of the management course" in Day, C. & Poster, C. (eds) *Educational Management Purposes and Practices.* Croom Helm.

FULLAN, M. (1982) *The Meaning of Educational Change.* Teachers College Press, New York.

HEWTON, E. (1987) *School-Focussed Staff Development.* Falmer Press.

HOLLY, P., JAMES, T. & YOUNG, J. (1987) *The Experience of TRIST: Practitioners' Views of INSET and Recommendations for the Future*. Final Report of Delta Project. Manpower Services Commission.

HOPKINS, P. (ed.) (1986) *In-Service Training and Educational Development Survey*. Croom Helm.

HOWEY, K.R. & JOYCE, B. (1978) "A Data base for future directions in in-service education". *Theory into Practice*, 17, pp 206-211.

HUBERMAN, A.M. & MILES, M.B. (1984) *Innovation Up Close: How School Improvement Works*. Plenum, New York.

JOYCE, B.R. & SHOWERS, B. (1980) "Improving in-service training: the messages of research". *Educational Leadership*, pp 379-385.

LORTIE, D.C. (1975) *Schoolteacher: a sociological study*. University of Chicago Press.

NISBETT, R.E. & ROSS, L. (1980) *Human inference: strategies and shortcomings of social judgement*. Prentice-Hall.

OLDROYD, P. & HALL, V. (1988) *Managing Professional Development and INSET*. NDCSMT, Bristol University School of Education.

PETRÁČEK, S. (1986) "In-Service Training of Teachers: Issues and Trends". *Information Review*, Vol. 10. European Information Centre of Charles University for Further Education of Teachers, Prague.

RADNOR, H. (1987) The Impact of the Introduction of GCSE at LEA and School Level. National Foundation for Education Research, Slough, UK.

RUDDUCK, J. (1981) *Making the Most of the Short In-Service Course*. Schools Council Working Paper 71. Methuen.

SHOWERS, B. (1985) "Teachers coaching teachers" *Educational Leadership*, pp 43-48.

STALLINGS, J. (1979) "Follow Through: A model for in-service teacher training." *Curriculum Inquiry*, 8, pp 163-181.

WALLACE, M. (1988) *Improving School Management Training: Towards a New Partnership*. NDCSMT, Bristol University School of Education.

4

Efficiency of Further Training of Teachers and Education Administrators

Viktor Onushkin
Union of Soviet Socialist Republics

The evaluation of the efficiency of the further training of teachers is an important and pressing problem. Along with an increase in the role of education in the life of society, due to the acceleration of scientific, technological and socio-economic progress, improving the quality of education and evaluating the efficiency of the work, training and further education of teachers also assume a greater importance.

In the conditions of perestroika, which affects all social life in the Soviet Union, deep changes are taking place in education. The 27th Congress of the Communist Party of the Soviet Union held in 1986 set up the task of building in this country a unified system of life-long education embracing all stages of education — pre-school, secondary, higher and post-diploma education. The solution of this problem is an indispensable condition of the realisation of the general strategy of the Communist Party of the USSR, which is aimed at the acceleration of the socio-economic development of the country, the democratisation of social life, the augmentation of the human factor and the spiritual growth of personality.

A number of important steps, directed at the perestroika of the general secondary and professional school, the specialised secondary school, higher education, and the further training and retaining of workers and specialists in industry and agriculture, have been taken in this country. In this respect a very special importance can be attributed to the decisions of the February 1988 plenary meeting of the Central Committee of the USSR Communist Party, which were directed at putting into practice the building of a unified system of life-long education and the decisive improvement of the quality of educational work in all parts of education.

The need for life-long education has a deep social determination. It is determined by the dynamic development of modern industry, its technology and technological processes, and changes in the content and forms of labour in the course of a scientific and technological revolution. The rapid growth in the volume of information in all spheres of science, technology and culture has led to the ageing of previously acquired knowledge. As a result, an objective need to renew and enrich previous training came into being.

The modern revolutionary stage in the development of Soviet society requires the full involvement of all citizens in the management of production and other spheres of social life. In turn, it assumes that people should adopt an active social position and acquire the knowledge and skills necessary for fulfilling various social and professional functions. Perestroika, acceleration of the socio-economic development of society, the democratisation of Soviet society and the reform of the political system based on self-government, glasnost, the development of the initiative of citizens, governing bodies, party, social organisations and labour collectives require on the part of every person a permanent creativity, a deep professionalism and a high spiritual culture.

Life-long education embracing all human life becomes one of the decisive factors of socio-economic progress, the condition for development of the personality in all aspects of its life and professional growth.

The perestroika of education in the USSR ought to favour the further development of the spiritual life of society.

The further training of teachers is one of the most important sub-systems of lifelong education. Research in the field of the further training of teachers in the USSR is carried out at the Research Institute of Adult Education of the USSR Academy of Pedagogical Sciences, which also co-ordinates the studies of various aspects of this problem in other research centres and higher learning institutions of the country.

The logic of research and development presupposes a certain sequence in setting up and solving problems. The development of typical programmes for educators in the system of further training institutes and faculties for teachers and education administrators has called for study of the real knowledge and skills of teachers, and the comparison of these data with the requirements facing the teacher in the solution of new educational challenges brought about by the speeding up of scientific, technological and socio-economic progress.

This comparison pointed to a need for research on the develpoment of professional profiles for various types of educators. This permitted the finding of weak points in the work patterns and previous training of teachers and suggested the measures aimed at eliminating these weaknesses. This was, in fact, the first research approach to the problem of the evaluation of the efficiency of further training.

Simultaneously, research on the structure of teaching as an activity and the professionally significant qualities of the teacher's personality was carried out.

As a result, the necessary courses for the retraining and further training of teachers were set up.

The development of new generations of educational programmes for the further training of teachers presented the researchers with the problem of integrating the preceding and subsequent cycles of further training. This led inevitably to approaching further training from the position of the concept of life-long education. In this case research on the relationship between classroom training in its various forms and self-education also becomes very important.

The research also led to defining more precisely the approaches to the problem of the efficiency of teachers' further training and the methods for measuring its efficiency.

As a result of going through a certain stage of further training a teacher has to be more ready to solve educational problems and take into account numerous conditions in the development of the region and the school as well as the peculiarities of the class and the individual student.

It is obvious that, by bearing in mind the many and continually changing conditions of the teacher's task, one can suggest two possible approaches to further training: whether by trying to give a teacher instructions and advice for all situations and constantly adding to and enriching them, which as experience shows is practically impossible, or by transferring the focus of further training to the development of the teacher's personality and the growth of his or her creative potential, so that the teacher can take necessary decisions in new situations. The practice and the research carried out shows that only creatively working teachers can take into account all the variety of changing conditions and in due course react to them in the working process. It is known that only a creative personality can educate another creative personality.

Thus, in the process of perostroika in the modern school the task of developing the creative teacher's potential during his or her training or further training period becomes of the first importance.

A comparative analysis of the practical experience gained in the training of teachers made it possible to suggest three main objectives of teacher education and self-education:

(1) filling in the blanks in the knowledge of a teacher;
(2) operative retraining of a teacher on account of changes in the content, forms and methods in the work of the school;
(3) increasing the level of a teacher's readiness for creative educational work and the independent solution of the numerous problems arising during the working process.

In the theory of life-long education of adults these main functions are respectively regarded as compensatory, adaptive and developing.

The further education of a teacher is first of all the process of his or her growth as a personality and a professional person, a process which can only occur in the working situation. However, the interdependency between such activity and the development of the personality of a teacher does not arise spontaneously; its efficiency is determined by a number of principal conditions. In particular, the teacher's professional growth takes place only when he or she has the opportunity:

(1) to occupy the position of an active participant in activities where the creative forces and capabilities are realised;

(2) to be included as a free, equal and responsible participant in the system of collective interpersonal relationships (including "teacher-students", "teacher-other teachers", "teacher-administrator", "teacher-parents", "teacher-social workers" etc.);

(3) to combine individual practical experience with a broad social and professional experience (e.g. to analyse and interpret personal experience from the point of view of theory and practice);

(4) to feel morally and socially responsible as a person and in relation to the quality of one's work.

From this point of view all the institutional forms of further training act, or ought to act, as establishments for assisting the professional growth of a teacher, organising the creative atmosphere among the members of the school staff, jointly solving the current problems of school life, giving a teacher the choice of numerous, flexible and dynamic forms of learning and stimulating his or her permanent professional growth and development. The inclusion of the teacher in a system of life-long education by means of a sub-system of further training is significant in the sense of perfecting the teacher's personality and also solving the problem of student training for life-long education.

As a sub-system, the further education of educators is responsible for providing the actualisation, modernisation and enrichment of professional, political, economical, legal, ecological and general cultural knowledge, and for forming the pedagogical mastery and realisation of the teacher's creative potential.

The system of further education of educators in the Soviet Union comprises a broad network of teachers' further education institutes, faculties of further training in the teachers' training colleges and universities, various scientific departments and regional methodological centres. These provide a compulsory quinquennial classroom course for every teacher, by helping teachers to prepare themselves to work with a new syllabus, by giving the teacher a choice of compulsory and optional courses, by organising a considerable number of workshops during the interstudy period and making a positive contribution to perfecting the professional mastery of educators.

However, stagnation processes in society affected the state of this sub-system of education and hindered the development of further training of educators.

The perestroika of the system of further training of educators on the basis of the principle of life-long education can be carried out while providing for the following conditions:

(1) the organic interdependence of organised education and self-education;
(2) the maximal satisfaction of the real needs of the teacher; the achievement of optimal interdependence between the social determination of the teacher's continuing training and his or her subjective capabilities;
(3) the variation and differentiation of teachers' further training at different stages of their professional activities, and self-reliance in choosing the content, forms, methods, duration and rate of their further training;
(4) the integration of basic and additional education, taking into account the differences and functional peculiarities.

In the present climate of the perestroika of education the objectives of the further training of educators subsume the development of the creative teacher's potential, the improvement of his or her personal qualities and professional knowledge and skills and the final prognostic aim — a considerable improvement in the quality of students' education.

The main practical problem which must be solved in the process of the further training of teachers is to define what can and must be contributed by that process to the development of a teacher's creative potential and to determine the conditions which influence a teacher's attitude to his profession, the development of his capabilities, his conceptual thinking and his general readiness to cope with the content, forms and methods of the modern educational process. As already noted, the creative potential formed in the process of the teacher's education realises itself in his activities. Therefore the study and evaluation of the efficiency of teacher education require the development of criteria and indicators which reflect the teacher's practical activities, namely:

(1) on the level of the teacher's social and professional activity;
(2) in the enrichment of his needs and interests;
(3) in the development of his knowledge as the basis of pedagogical thinking;
(4) in the development of the skills needed in order to analyse concrete pedagogical situations, put forward new pedagogical tasks, work out the constructive solutions of those tasks and adequately evaluate the effectiveness of these actions.

The experimental research work on the motivation of the social and professional activities of teachers in city and country schools was carried out at the Research Institute of General Adult Education of the USSR Academy of Pedagogical Sciences. This consisted of studying the education and self-education needs of both young and experienced teachers and the pedagogical conditions for the professional improvement and development of the creative activity of teachers and other groups of educators (principals and moral educators) in the system of teachers' further training.

In order to study the above-mentioned issues a complex of diagnostic and constructive methods included:

— methods for studying teachers' social and professional activity;
— materials on the organisation of "the young teachers' school";
— methods for studying the needs of teachers at different levels of mastery;
— experimental programmes for organising lectures, seminars and workshops at the institutes of further education for teachers and the district methodological centres;
— methods of analysis and self-analysis of the level of theoretical and practical readiness of a teacher for the creative solving of pedagogical problems.

The research carried out at the Institute was comprehensive and interdisciplinary.

While studying the socio-pedagogical problems of the development of the professional and social activity of the teachers, the main task was to study the professional motivation and satisfaction of teachers in city and country schools at different stages in their careers.

The analysis, based on questionnaires, interviews etc., showed a discrepancy between the teacher's professional satisfaction and his or her working satisfaction. In the latter area the insufficient preparedness of the teacher to deal with difficult situations and a disposition to solve them by relying on personal experience rather than on general professional knowledge and skills was found. It should be noted that further training does not lead to considerable changes in that process. A discrepancy between the ideals of self-education and its real process, its domination by narrow professional problems, was also found. On the basis of experimental work with young teachers the most efficient forms of post-college education for this stage were suggested.

In the course of studying the development of the teacher's psychological and pedagogical needs at different stages of his professional development, it was found that the most important factors influencing the teacher's creative potential are:

— the general orientation of a teacher's personality in the sphere of professional development and self-education;
— the level of general culture;
— professional knowledge and skills;
— individual peculiarities and the individual style of professional development.

The possibility of the creative realisation of the personality in activities and relationships with students and colleagues is at the centre of the system of the teacher's value orientations. Significant differences in the teachers' needs, depending on length of service, were not recorded.

The study of further training processes for teachers of different subjects showed that the efficiency of further training is directly dependent on how a teacher can deal with pedagogical problems: on the organisation of group and individual research work directed at the exchange of experience; on the analysis of conditions for the practical use of scientific results and advanced pedagogical experience; on the development of the teacher's skills of self-analysis and the critical evaluation of his activities and those of other teachers; on the differentiation of further training through development, parallel with the general courses, of a system of special courses and workshops answering the content and character of the teaching, the experience of the teacher and the stage of his or her work.

Hence, during the experimental work the main conditions in the formation of professional mastery are specified and the role and significance of special courses, workshops, methodological tasks and video recordings of lessons for the improvement of the most important aspects of teaching are determined.

In a number of subject areas the characteristic work patterns of master teachers (those obtaining high results in educating their students) were determined, along with their needs, interests and motives for further training. The content of certain types of problem task aimed at the development of the teacher's professional and pedagogical thinking, analytical skills and self-analysis were validated.

In the future we have to develop and experimentally test a methodology for perfecting and developing the mastery of teaching.

Work on determining the significance and content of simulation games at further training courses for educators is being carried out, and the methodology of organising simulation games at the institutes for the further training of teachers is being developed.

In the course of the study the factors influencing development of the creative activity of educators in different parts of the system of further training were determined; the pedagogical conditions contributing to the development of creative initiatives among educators on the further training courses were clarified, and concrete methods of simulating professional self-reliance and initiative were developed.

Research on improving the professional skills of school administrators in the system of further training is also carried out in the Institute. The level of the professional skills of school administrators has been studied and their needs for further improvement have been analysed. It was found that the administrative skills of school management, as a component of teaching, involve the fusion of practical action with interdisciplinary theoretical knowledge. Therefore one can speak about the compulsory character of the theoretical component of practical classes and the adequate methodological and theoretical training of students. It can be accomplished at lectures and seminars and also through self-education.

This research showed that the setting up of didactic aims and the development of a system of practical classes is determined by the following circumstances:

— the modern social requirement for school administrators in the system of further training to support perestroika at the school level;
— the personal and professional needs of school administrators to perfect their administrative skills;
— the content and structure of the professional functions of school administrators;
— the logic of management activities acting as a sequence of periodically repetitive management cycles;
— the level of administrative skills acquired by school administrators before the beginning of the course.

The process of perfecting administrative skills can consist of the following stages:

— the stimulation of interest in the improvement of management activities and the nurture of positive motives for learning;
— filling up the blanks, modernising and deepening the theoretical knowledge on which this skill is based;
— acquiring knowledge about the operational structure of complicated management skills and concrete ways of action;
— acting according to a pattern;
— acting in new situations;
— doing creative tasks.

The complex multi-stage character of the process of improving management skills calls for an increase in the ratio of practical classes in the system for various forms of teaching.

In the development of the creative aspect of management by the school principal in the practical classes an important part is played by specific methods of teaching when a student becomes an active member of the educational process and participates in a creative search for the solutions to management problems.

The methods consist of the analysis of concrete management situations, the development of management activity projects for different spheres of school life, simulation games etc. In further training practice these methods are usually called active since they are based on the organisation of the goal-directed, active, intellectual and practical activities of students.

The use of active methods of teaching changes the role of students in the practical classes: from being the object of teaching they transform not only into active subjects of teaching, but also become researchers of management activities and of their own practical experience. When this system of teaching is used, the role of the teacher on the course also changes. The teacher is not only the source of new knowledge and an educator-advisor but also becomes a researcher, an expert, a referee in discussions who, together with the students, looks for a solution to management problems and predicts the outcome.

The main idea running through all the research carried out in the field of further training for educators is that of improving the efficiency of these activities. As already mentioned, the consideration of further training in the general context of life-long education permits us to look in a new way at evaluating efficiency.

The task of evaluating the efficiency of the teaching in general is a very important and difficult one. The solution to this problem will allow us to locate on a solid basis the evaluation of the efficiency of the further training of educators which is, in fact, that of increasing the efficiency of teaching as the result of further training.

As in all other spheres, the efficiency of teaching is measured through results or the increase of results. However, in the field of education not only quantitative but also qualitative indicators of work efficiency play an important role.

As complex indicators of the teacher's task, efficiency can be attributed to the quality of the educational process and the level of students' education. These indicators can be observed and to some extent measured. Their comparison before and after the process of further training can be used as the basis for the evaluation of the efficiency of further training.

An important indicator of the evaluation of the efficiency of further training is the estimation of the satisfaction of the participants. However, there is a considerable subjective element in this estimation and we cannot fully rely on it. The main thing is the results of the teacher's or school administrator's work.

The efficiency of the teacher's work can also be assessed by measuring the efficiency of students' work after they leave school and extracting from it the educational factor. Theoretically, in this way the measurement of the efficiency of pedagogical work is possible in terms of "cost indicators". But this is a postponed effect. Its measurement is important not only for establishing "feedback" to an actual teacher or school but mainly for improving activities in the sphere of education in general, including the sub-system of further training.

It should be noted that, since we regard the development of the teacher's creative potential as the main objective of further training and as a part of life-long education, the task of measuring the efficiency of the further training of educators consists to a large extent in measuring an increase of creative potential as a result of the further training process.

Hence, one can speak about the necessity for both theoretical and practical developments in regard to the problem of measuring the level of creative potential and the conditions for its full actualisation.

79

This problem requires a comprehensive interdisciplinary approach involving the efforts of psychologists, educators, sociologists, economists, management specialists etc., and the application from various fields of science and development of new methods of investigation. A large amount of work needs to be done in this field. This is one of the key problems of the concept of life-long education. It is worth serious attention on the part of researchers and through discussions at this conference.

TOPICS FOR DISCUSSION:

(1) What is the creative potential of educators?
(2) When is its development and full realisation possible?
(3) What are the criteria, indicators and methods of evaluation of the efficiency of the educator's work?
(4) What are the criteria, indicators and methods for evaluating the efficiency of the further training of educators?
(5) What are the criteria, indicators and methods for evaluating the educator's creative potential?

5

Research into the Further Education of Teachers in the German Democratic Republic

Helmut Stolz
German Democratic Republic

SUMMARY

Research on inservice training in the German Democratic Republic (GDR) serves first of all the effective planning, organization and preparation of decisions by educational authorities for the inservice training of teachers and educators.

In the 1960s and 70s the content and methods of inservice training were researched. In the 1970s and 80s the training of educational ability and the modification of behaviour by means of award-bearing and training courses became the focal point — the results of which are described. These served increasingly to test out different forms of inservice training for teachers, forms which may be also used in other forms of inservice training.

At present an analysis is being prepared of the inservice training of teachers and educators at the level of the county, the district and the school. This is looking into the relationship between inservice training and the social climate, the relationship between inservice training and work, the possibilities of differentiated and specialised inservice training for particular courses and situations, the effectiveness of the exchange of experience as a means of inservice training, the role of the head teacher as an inservice trainer and the verification of centrally devised programmes and recommendations.

1. RESEARCH IN THE GDR

Research into the further education of teachers (INSET) in the GDR was first carried out at the beginning of the 1970s. It was soon discovered that the integration of the research with that into the initial training of teachers resulted in the specifics of further education not being given their justified attention.

Further education has to build on the results of initial training, but these are so different and change to such an extent in the course of practical experience that, although the unity of initial training and further education should be retained as a methodological principle, it must not lead to an underestimation of the specifics of further education.

Research into the further education of teachers was, and is, directed at improving the conception, preparation, planning and didactic-methodological content, as well as the organisation, of further education, and at creating the conditions for raising the quality of these attributes.

The research project, ''The content and choice of further education,'' led to a choice of direction and material aids which proved to be an important basis for the effective long-term planning of further education. The main objective of this project was to establish guidelines for selecting the content of further education, as well as laying down recommendations and programmes to be published centrally. The following guidelines were elaborated, based on the social demands made on the further education of teachers in the GDR:

(1) demands and tasks which arise from trends developing within society;
(2) the personality development of the teacher;
(3) the general education to be passed on and its training potential, bearing in mind the real results of education and training;
(4) the political knowledge and the pedagogical-psychological abilities and knowledge that a teacher needs in order to overcome the tasks facing him or her;

82

(5) understanding problems and general development trends in science and technology, as well as in culture and the arts;

(6) the results of previous education and further education.

The research project, "On the didactic-methodological planning of further education," summarised important preconditions for its effectiveness. The results were passed into theoretical work as well as practical work in further education and the areas researched included:

— the planning of lectures and seminars (Martius, 1972);
— the introduction of teaching experience into further education (Wohlert, 1972; Kreysig, 1983; T. Hoedt, 1985);
— the use of educational aids as a subject and means of further education (Haak, 1983; M. Hoedt, 1983);
— the elaboration of aids to studying as supportive material (Schoop, 1978);
— the planning and use of radio programmes for the further education of teachers (Hohlfeld, 1981).

Results from the research project, "On private study by teachers" (Machut, 1980), were used to influence directly the content and extent of the recommended literature, as well as the availability and preparation of pedagogical, psychological and methodological literature on classroom teaching and the use of specialist libraries by teachers.

Research projects from earlier years, which were partly in the form of dissertations, were devoted to further education in the Soviet Union (Mauckisch, 1974; Bernsdorff, 1976), further education in the form of specialist circles (Babeck, 1969), and in postgraduate studies (Schubert, 1966), as well as the historical development of further education courses and the consequences for their planning (Wölk, 1977).

2. TRAINING COURSES AS A FORM OF FURTHER EDUCATION

In the sixties, research into teacher performance was begun. This dealt at first with the important moments of teacher behaviour, as experienced by the pupils, with encouraging behavioural features by the teacher, and finally with the analysis of the variable personality features of teachers which encourage success (Grassel, 1974 and 1982; Klinker, 1975).

This led almost inevitably to re-thinking how teacher behaviour could be changed by schooling and training.

Since teacher-pupil relationships are of decisive importance for the effectiveness of the teacher, special attention was given to the "guidance"-behaviour of teachers, or more simply to the question of how to lead. On the basis of a knowledge of the subjective pre-conditions and behavioural features, research was conducted into how it was possible to enable teachers to develop, by means of socio-psychological training, educationally effective leadership behaviour. Appropriate courses were directed towards overcoming negative behavioural patterns by encouraging teacher-personality variables such as understanding, friendliness, consistency and perseverance (Kessel, 1976 and 1984).

Theoretical and experimental research, running in parallel, was aimed at strengthening the psychological and pedagogical abilities of teachers and student-teachers (Ecke, 1981; Flach, 1986; Fuhrmann, 1982; Rönsch, 1982; Rückwarth, 1984).

The studies also looked critically at previous experience of training, knowledge and techniques in capitalist countries. It was shown that, as a result of largely different bases and socially relevant aims — to the point of the often bewailed "lack of theoretical foundation" (Fricke and Thiele, 1983), these conceptions of training were of little use to us. Critical voices became increasingly louder (Lajewski, 1984).

Exercise and training programmes were created which were determined by the objectives of socialist education. These took into consideration the specific demands made on the specialist subject lessons in the socialist school, as well as on the teacher, and were aimed at improving certain components of their teaching abilities (Stolz, 1984 and 1986). As a special form of further education, programmes were tested with the objective of enabling the teacher to overcome educationally difficult situations (Mayer, 1988) and the planning of eventful, interesting literature lessons (Brunkow, 1986), as well as on the formation of the ability to imagine historical situations by junior school pupils (Wahlmann, 1986).

When deciding the content of these courses we paid attention to the practical demands of schools, the subjective needs of the participants and the necessity of deepening and reactivating their pedagogical and psychological knowledge in a planned way.

The following methods and procedures have proved themselves to be useful in our training courses:

— controversy lectures to motivate the participants, but also to reactivate and deepen their knowledge;
— discussions with oral and written decisions on the basis of theses, statements, and assertions, which are provided by the seminar leader, as well as teaching situations which have been experienced and described by participants, in addition to problem and conflict situations;
— private study with the possibility of looking at the problems of thought-out statements, and of refuting them as a method of reaching an own standpoint;
— role playing;
— the analysis, comparison and assessment of their own and other people's behaviour, or suggested decisions by other participants, with both oral and written suggestions;
— the derivation from collective knowledge of personal maxims, rules, behavioural techniques and strategies as well as assignments to reinforce the acquired teacher-activity in the ensuing practice;
— sound casette and video recordings as the basis of collective discussion of their own and other people's behaviour.

As a result of carrying out the training course many times under test conditions, the following results can be asserted:

(1) it is possible in relatively short intensive courses to reactivate and extend pedagogical and psychological knowledge related to the topic and its environment, so that theoretical statements become of personal importance and are acquired and recognised as necessary for the solution of practical pedagogical problems. This leads to a more exact picture by the teacher of him- or herself, since the participant can differentiate more carefully than previously his own pedagogical experience, activity and results;

(2) in such courses variations of possible actions can be worked out, discussed and exercised as a means of leading to the overcoming of pedagogical situations with relative certainty;

(3) the acquired behaviour maxims, personal assignments and individual programmes for the maximum benefit of the pedagogical activity are, to a high degree, put into practice when the teacher returns to the classroom;

(4)   from the point of view of the participating teachers, they find the courses impressive because of the high demands made on them, the studious atmosphere, the relatively high degree of private study and the close connection between the acquired theory and the practical needs of the teachers. Despite the intensity of the course and the heavy work-load during the course the teachers often remark that they would voluntarily take part in similar courses (if that were possible) although at first they were rather sceptical towards the high demands of the active study;

(5)   training courses lead to the experiencing of a higher degree of subjective security, and in comparison with previous successful methodological approaches, almost all participants believe that the transfer effect will operate in other pedagogical situations apart from the ones exercised;

(6)   it has been proved experimentally that the pedagogical situation, which for the teacher is at the same time an assignment, problem, and decision situation, is, in relation to its size, suited to the formation or stabilisation of pedagogical abilities;

(7)   the results of the training course are particularly effective afterwards on the teaching when several teachers from the same school (12 - 18 teachers) take part, and head teachers, as well as specialist advisors, taking into account their responsibilities, support the stabilisation of the results required by the teachers. If the participants in a training course know that they will later lead a group in the programme which they have completed, then their active participation is especially high.

In other experiments it was shown that "extended" training courses (in which the participants work through a particular programme over a whole school year) are effective, but are regarded by most participants as harder in work load and time consumed.

On the basis of our empirical experimental research on the formation of components of pedagogical knowledge, it was concluded that both intensive and extensive training and exercising courses are possible, necessary and effective. However, mainly for reasons of personnel (the number of trained group-leaders available for relatively small exercise groups) they can only be carried out on a limited scale in the further education of teachers. Exercises in the "normal" seminars are essentially more broadly effective (Slomma, 1986), but do not lead to the changes in the abilities of individual teachers which are aimed at in training courses or at least begun there.

86

Thus, in further education the main attention must be directed to increasing those parts of the seminar which exercise abilities in order to make the seminars more effective. At the same time the training courses, as here depicted, will retain their important place.

3. ON THE ANALYSIS OF THE PRACTICE OF FURTHER EDUCATION AND ITS CONSEQUENCES

A practical analysis which is at present being carried out by the Central Institute for Further Education is intended to examine the effectiveness of further education in specific areas such as the town or country district. The main methods used for this are open-ended and standardised interviews and the observation of lessons in all the schools and further education meetings in the district, as well as an analysis of documentation. The following questions are central to the enquiry.

3.1 What is the relationship between the atmosphere among the staff and the demand for further education?

The demand for further education by teachers is not dependent primarily on the time available to the individual teacher. A greater effect is that of the collective atmosphere which prevails in the school in relation to the level of attainment of the individual teacher, which in turn is strongly influenced by the personality of the head teacher. At the same time, it is obvious that a decisive role is played by previous experience of the possibility of influencing important problems in the planning of school life (see Stolz, 1988).

Decisive above all else in influencing the demand for further education is the degree of identification with (a) the demands made on the teacher by socialist society and (b) the teaching profession as a whole, including the actual experience of exercising responsibility towards children and young people. However, open and friendly criticism and assistance are also important in this connection. Hints from head teachers, specialist advisors and other experienced teachers, based on analyses of the pedagogical work of the individual, his or her attitude to the modification of behaviour patterns and deepening knowledge, but above all the exchange of experiences, very often lead to private study and mutual observation of lessons, as examples of further education which take place outside formal further education and which mostly remain anonymous. But the contradiction between the specialist knowledge and pedagogical-psychological demands of teaching on the one hand, and the personal capacities of the teacher on the other, is the most decisive determinant as regards motivation for further education. Deficiencies of which one has become conscious are more easily eliminated when one is certain that they can be reduced or compensated for extensively from one's own abilities, or by means of collective assistance. Extensive study of the relevant literature is mostly (especially for young and male teachers) the result of specific assignments taken up as voluntary holiday tasks.

3.2 How far can effectiveness be raised by differentiated and practical further education?
The interest of teachers in further education has increased noticeably since compulsory courses in further education were for the most part replaced by a differentiated offer of compulsory choices and optional events. The interest is particularly high when theoretically demanding lectures and seminars are linked with directed observation of lessons in their own school as well as private study, and where the results are closely linked to practical teaching. With the introduction into all classes of the ten-year general polytechnical secondary school in the GDR, and of new syllabi now in progress, the theoretical questions of general education are being closely experienced by teachers. From this arises a strong demand, commonly a kind of ''technical pressure'' for further education, which is not only related to the acquisition of subject specialist- and teaching methodological-knowledge, but to psychological and pedagogical questions of personality development in general (Stolz, 1988b).

3.3 How are experience and exchange of experiences made effective as a means of further education?
Pedagogical experience has always been either a stimulant for further education or a hindrance thereto; the latter, if the experience is mainly negative, and if treated as such, can even lead to a wish to change professions. Experience has always been an important source for the subjective acquisition of knowledge as well as the decisive basis for the collective and individual activity of teachers. Thus, it is clearly of great important to enable individual experience to be considered theoretically and to make it useful in this way for the future educational work of the teacher.

At the same time, the need by teachers to exchange experiences in the context of further education has also grown. This only becomes really effective, however, when the process of the origin and cause of the experience, and the conditions surrounding it, are the centre of consideration. Using the experience of other teachers is not necessarily effective simply because someone identifies him- or herself with that experience. This only happens when the teacher is made to think deeply about his behaviour, its causes and results, the sense of the pedagogical experience of the other person and, as a result of individual stimulation, to enrich and change his thinking in the interests of more satisfying teaching. In this sense experience is the product of a process of re-examining and, at the same time, stabilising one's pedagogical abilities. Naturally, the effect of exchanging experiences is optimised by comparison with previous experience and leads to theoretical understanding.

It has been shown that, in the process of establishing pedagogical experience, stimulating "experience-reports" — often from 25 to 40 pages long and called "educational readings" — given before colleagues can lead to a deepened concern with theoretical aspects and knowledge. But "educational readings" have also contributed to the elaboration of conceptual material and the enrichment of specialist subject teaching. Unfortunately, this treasure trove of experience has not yet been sufficiently generalised by pedagogical theory and put to use (see Bauer, 1988).

3.4 How does a head teacher approach his responsibility for further education?
In the GDR education system the responsibility of the head teacher for the standard of educational work, especially in the classroom, has absolute priority. This includes responsibility for the continuous further education of each of his members of staff. In official state documents the qualification of teachers — in both initial training and further education — is regarded as a key to the further development of education itself.

Responsibility for the further education of teachers in any school can only be correctly considered by a leader of the collective who, as a subject specialist, seeks to improve his own abilities, which are then recognised so that his competence is stabilised and improved. This is being achieved by an increasing number of school heads, in so far as they establish a "regime" in common with their experienced teachers and representatives of the political organisations in the school (Party, trade union and youth organisation), which ensures the democratic participation in decision-making and responsibility of all the teachers and, to a large extent, of the pupils too. Of course, the other day-to-day priorities, especially in administration and organisation, are a hurdle for the individual head teacher in this connection.

If the head teacher manages to conduct his own lessons well or excellently, to lead meetings of staff which develop their personality and to spend at least half his time with others (teachers, pupils, elected representatives of the pupils and parents), then he will at the same time be conducting a highly important and effective programme of further education. This particularly involves the

89

regular observation of lessons, extra-curricular organised events and their evaluation (three to five lesson-observations a week is common, while some heads manage, temporarily, to reach ten a week). The main object of lesson observation is to assist the observed teacher to achieve better standards and also to help him in the assessment of his own work, which leads naturally to maxims for self-improvement.

3.5 How do the central recommendations and further education stand the test?
The recommendations laid down by the Central Institute for Further Education of Teachers and Educators for further education courses influence the choice of themes and the emphasis placed in the advisory meetings of specialist subject teachers — one of which exists in each district — as well as the theoretical-practical discussions in the schools, but especially in the specialist circles, in the educational council, and in certain trade union meetings. They start from the demands of the schools, the state of scientific knowledge and an analysis of school work. Also worked out by the Central Institute, and approved by the Ministry of Education, is a programme for further education in the political, pedagogical-psychological, subject specialist and teaching method areas which determines the content of courses and the themes of individual meetings held in the districts. The precondition for these, however, is that new scientific knowledge is presented and old ideas are put to debate, refuted or reconciled. At the same time the lecturers, seminar leaders and participating teachers must be stimulated into injecting into discussion their own knowledge and experiences. The greater the ability of the "further educator" (the lecturer, seminar leader etc.), the more he is likely to use the centrally presented themes — compulsory, limited choice and optional — in an original and independent way.

Further education which takes place in the context of school work and which is decisively affected by a concern with lesson content and methodology influences the level of seminars and training sessions. The effect on the everyday planning of practical educational work is, naturally, difficult to prove, since it is affected by so many other factors. What can be shown is that the central orientation affects the attitude of the teacher to further education and his or her orientation towards it.

The results of the practical analysis now in progress will be enriched by the examination in other regions and districts of the GDR of aspects of the problems there presented. They have the aim of leading to a new concept for the content and organisational planning of further education in the 90s which will enable the Ministry of Education to make decisions which take into account social and especially scientific-technological trends. In short, scientific research will lead to official decision making. In order to give such important decisions a scientific basis and thus improve further education, we have sought to co-ordinate existing results with scientific research.

In addition, the following projects are at present in progress.

(1) The teacher as subject and object of further education, which is an integrated part of his activity. Here we are particularly concerned with the directed use of the knowledge of the psychology of adults, as well as the psychology of the personality and teacher activity as means of stressing the subjective element in the teacher's further education. This should lead to suggestions for the content and didactic-methodological design of further education.

(2) Improving pedagogic abilities through further education has three aspects:

    (a) pedagogic ability is mainly stabilised in the preparation, arrangement and "post mortems" of lessons, as well as in lesson observation. However, the possibilities and connections necessary to maximise training and self-training in this area must be researched;

    (b) pedagogical ability will, in the future, be improved by specific training courses for teachers in the various school subjects and according to their various experience. Here we must check how the growth of teaching ability shows itself in practical work in the classroom, and whether its sources can be more accurately distinguished. This could have considerable consequences for the planning of further education. The development of teaching abilities on a broader basis and with greater stability is intended by the production of materials such as orientation aids, handouts, articles and training programmes;

    (c) teaching ability — even if it is of a special nature — must be shown also by the staff involved in further education. This can also be exercised in specific training courses, in which university-level pedagogics and the psychology of adults play an important role.

(3) The history of further education as a source of maximising present-day further education.

The main consideration is the documentation of features and processes, as well as the production and depiction of preconditions, conditions and connections which have contributed to the development of the further education of teachers.

4. PROBLEMS

We are of the opinion that the following questions need more research as well as international co-operation in research.

(1) In the light of developmental trends in the differing social systems, what should be the content of further education? Despite all the social differences and special national features, as well as individual interests, the educating of teachers to enable them to educate young people as active representatives of world-wide peace must be in the foreground. This task is increased by the necessity of dealing with other global problems such as the environment and the ending of mass hunger and illiteracy. The education of a personality conscious of his or her responsibility is of all-round pedagogical concern which must, above all else, also determine the content of further education for teachers.

(2) How can the motivation and demand for further education be developed into a life-long need and the methods of supporting the self-education of teachers be made more effective?

With respect to the specific responsibility of teachers for the education of children and youth, we should not pay overdue attention to this or that quality, ability, or skill, but instead concentrate our attention on the ability of the teacher to improve his own personality.

(3) How can the effectiveness of the "teacher of the teacher" (Diesterweg) be improved?

With all due respect to self-education and self-improvement by the teacher, even with the most intensive efforts the active classroom teacher cannot acquire all that science regards as new and necessary knowledge for the education of young people. Scientists, and especially successful teachers and school officials who are involved in the further education of teachers, have to help teachers to find its more general characteristic features. The

92

effectiveness of the teacher's personality is, under present-day conditions, potentially decisive in raising the effectiveness of further education. This also requires more research.

5. QUESTIONS FOR DISCUSSION

(1) What determines the needs for inservice training of teachers? What determining factors should be strengthened?

(2) To what extent can the school itself be used as a place for inservice training?

(3) How can the effectiveness of the "teachers of teachers" in the different forms of inservice training be strengthened?

(4) Which effects of inservice training become directly evident and provable in the practical work of the teachers?

(5) What are the possibilities and limits of training and award-bearing courses for teachers and educators?

LITERATURE

BABECK, H.J. (1969) Weiterbildung der Lehrer in Fachzirkeln — unter besonderer Berücksichtigung des Faches Geographie (Inservice training of teachers in subject groups — with special representation of the subject Geography). Diss. A, Pädagogische Hochschule, Dresden.

BAUER, M. (1987) Zum pädagogisch-methodischen Ideengehalt hervorragender pädagogischer Lesungen über den Chemieunterricht aus den Jahren 1981 bis 1985 (On the pedagogic-methodic ideas contained in excellent pedagogic lectures on chemistry-teaching of the years 1981 to 1985). Diss. B, Akademie der Pädagogischen Wissenschaften der DDR.

BERNSDORFF, W. (1976) Untersuchungen zur Entwicklung der Weiterbildung der Lehrer in der Estnischen SSR unter besonderer Berücksichtigung der Qualifizierung im Fach Körpererziehung (Studies on the development of the inservice training of teachers in the Esthonian SSR under special representation of the qualification in the subject physical education). Diss. A, Wilhem-Pieck-Universitat, Rostock.

BRUNKOW, E. (1986) Entwicklung der Fähigkeit der Lehrer zum erlebnisfördernden Umgang mit künstlerischer Literatur im Unterricht (Development of the ability of teachers for the eventful use of artistic literature in lessons). Diss. A, Pädagogische Hochschule, Potsdam.

ECKE, P. 1981) Untersuchungen zum pädagogischen Konnen (Studies on pedagogic ability). Volk und Wissen Volkseigener Verlag, Berlin (Beiträge zur Pädagogik, Heft 25).

FLACH, H. (1986) Zur Entwicklung des pädagogischen Könnens in der Lehrerausbildung (On the development of pedagogic ability in the training of teachers). Volk und Wissen Volkseigener Verlag. Berlin.

FRICKE, R. & THIELE, H. (1983) Trainingskurse zur Veränderung des Lehrerverhaltens (Training courses for changing the behaviour of teachers). In: Fricke, R., Kury, H. (Hrg.): Erzieher-verhaltenstraining, Braunschweig.

FUHRMANN, E. (1982) Über ein Verfahren zur quantitativen Erfassung wesentlicher Merkmale des Unterrichts (About a method for the quantitative registration of important characteristics of lessons). In: Jahrbuch 1982, Akademie der Pädagogischen Wissenschaften der DDR. Volk und Wissen Volkseigener Verlag Berlin 1982, S. 314 ff.

GRASSEL, H. (1970) Probleme und Methoden der Lehrerforschung (Problems and methods of research on teachers). In: Ergebnisse und Probleme der Psychologie. Berlin (34), S. 9 ff.

— (1982) Zu einigen Problemen und Ergebnissen der Arbeit der Rostocker Forschungsgruppe "Lehrertätigkeit — Lehrerpersönlichkeit — Lehrergesundheit" (On some problems and results of the work of the Rostock research group "Work of the teacher — personality of the teacher — health of the teacher"). In: Erziehungswissenschaftliche Beiträge der Wilhelm-Pieck-Universität, Rostock, (6), S. 17 ff.

HAAK, M. (1983) Zur Arbeit mit Unterrichtsmitteln in der Weiterbildung der Lehrer (On the work with teaching aids in the inservice training of teachers). In: Erkenntnisse, Erfahrungen, Berichte, ZIW, S. 40-49.

HELLER, E. (1983) Untersuchungen zur historischen Entwicklung der Weiterbildung der Kindergärtnerinnen in der DDR — 1945 bis Ende der 60er Jahre (Investigations on the historic development of the inservice training of kindergarten teachers in the GDR — 1945 to the end of the 1960's). Diss. A, Humboldt-Universität, Berlin.

HOEDT, W. (1983) Einige Anregungen zum weiteren Nachdenken über Fragen der Konzeption und des Einsatzes von Unterrichtsmitteln in Lehrveranstaltungen der Lehrerweiterbildung (Some suggestions for the further thinking about questions of the conception and the use of teaching aids in lectures and seminars of inservice training). In: Erkenntnisse, Erfahrungen, Berichte, ZIW, S. 50-55.

— (1985) Pädagogische Erfahrungen — Gegenstand der Weiterbildungsforschung (Pedagogic experiences — subject of research on inservice training). In: Erkenntnisse, Erfahrungen, Berichte, ZIW, S. 20-24.

HOHLFELD, T. (1981) Anforderungen an Rundfunksendungen für die Weiterbildung der Lehrer (Demands on broadcasting-lectures for the inservice training of teachers). Diss. A, Martin-Luther-Universitat Halle, Wittenberg.

KESSEL, W. (1976) Zur Theorie und Praxis des Führungsverhaltens der Lehrer in der sozialistischen Schule (On theory and practice of the guidance-behaviour of teachers in the socialist school). Diss. B, Karl-Marx-Universitat, Leipzig.

— (1984) Probleme und Ergebnisse der psychologischen Lehrerforschung (Problems and results of psychological research on teachers). In: Lehrerpersönlichkeit — Lehrertätigkeit — Lehrergesundheit. Ludwigsfelde, S. 4 ff.

KLINKER, E. (1975) Pädagogisch schwierige Situationen und ihre Bewältigung durch Lehrer (Difficult pedagogic situations and their solution by the teachers). Wissenschaftliche Zeitschrift der Universitat Rostock. Gesellschafts-und sprachwissenschaftliche Reihe, Heft 10, S. 877 ff.

KREYSIG, U. (1983) Untersuchungen zur inhaltlichen und didaktisch- methodischen Gestaltung von Erfahrungsberichten in der Weiterbildung der Lehrer in Kursen (Investigations on the content and didactic-methodic design of reports on experience in inservice training courses). Diss. A, Pädagogische Hochschule, Potsdam.

LAJEWSKI, E.M. (1984) Zum bürgerlichen Lehrertraining in der BRD, Eine Literaturstudie (On bourgeois teacher training in the FRG. A study of the literature). Diss. B, Wilhelm-Pieck-Universität, Rostock.

MACHUT, G. (1980) Zur Lenkbarkeit des Literaturstudiums der Lehrer auf dem Gebiet der pädagogischen und psychologischen Literatur durch zentrale Empfehlungen (On guidance for teachers in their study of centrally recommended pedagogical and psychological literature). Diss. A, Pädagogische Hochschule, Potsdam.

MARTIUS, W. (1972) Das Seminar in der Weiterbildung der Lehrer — seine Funktion bei der Entwicklung der Lehrerpersönlichkeit und Voraussetzungen und Bedingungen seiner effektiven Gestaltung (The seminar in the inservice training of teachers — its function for the development of the personality of the teacher and conditions of its effective planning). Diss. A, Pädagogische Hochschule, Dresden.

MAUCKISCH, H. (1974) Die Selbstbildung als Prinzip und Hauptform der Weiterbildung von Lehrern in der Ukrainischen SSR (Self-education as principle and principal method of inservice training of teachers in the Ukrainian SSR). Diss. A, Pädagogische Hochschule, Potsdam.

MAYER, G. (1988) Vervollkommnung pädagogischen Könnens durch Befähigungskurse — ein Beitrag zur Verbesserung der pädagogischen und psychologischen Weiterbildung von Pädagogen (Perfection of pedagogic ability by training courses — a contribution to the improvement of the pedagogic and psychological inservice training of teachers). Diss. A, Pädagogische Hochschule, Erfurt/Mühlhausen.

RÖNSCH, M. (1982) Untersuchungen zur effektiven Befähigung von Lehrern, problemhaft zu unterrichten (Investigations on the effective qualification of teachers to teach in a problem-oriented manner). Diss. A, Akademie der Pädagogischen Wissenschaften der DDR, Berlin.

RÜCKWARTH, J. (1984) Zur Befähigung von Lehrerstudenten und Lehrern zur Führung und psychologischen Analyse des Erkenntnisprozesses der Schüler unter besonderer Berücksichtigung des schöpferischen Denkens durch Problemlösen (On the qualification of teacher-students and teachers for the guidance and psychological analysis of the perception-process of pupils with special emphasis on the creative thinking by the solving of problems). Diss. B, Akademie der Pädagogischen Wissenschaften der DDR.

SCHOOP, U. (1978) Anforderungen an die didaktisch-methodische Gestaltung von Studienhilfen fur die Weiterbildung der Lehrer, umgesetzt am Beispiel von Studienhilfen fur die Weiterbildung der Staatsbürgerkundelehrer (Demands on the didactic-methodic planning of study-guidelines for the inservice training of teachers, accomplished on the example of guidelines for the inservice training of teachers for Civics). Diss. A, Pädagogische Hochschule, Potsdam.

SCHUBERT, L. (1966) Die Bestimmung der inhaltlichen Aufgabe bei der postgradualen Weiterbildung von Musiklehrern in allgemeinbildenden POS als ein Beitrag zur Verwirklichung des Gesetzes über das einheitliche sozialistische Bildungs-system (The task of defining the content for the postgraduate qualification of music teachers in polytechnical schools as a contribution to the realization of the law on the unified socialist educational system). Diss. A, DPZI, Berlin.

95

SLOMMA, R. (1986) Seminare in der Weiterbildung müssen zur Verbesserung der pädagogischen Arbeit anregen (Seminars in inservice training must stimulate the improvement of pedagogic work). In: Pädagogische Forschung, Heft 2/1986, S. 59 ff.

STOLZ, H. (1984) Pädagogisches Können — Bedingung und Resultat erfolgreicher Lehrertätigkeit (Pedagogic ability — condition and result of successful work of teachers). In: Jahrbuch 1984, Akademie der Pädagogischen Wissenschaften der DDR. Volk and Wissen Volkseigener Verlag, Berlin, S. 111 ff.

— (1986) Vervollkommnung pädagogischen Könnens durch Weiterbildung (Perfection of pedagogic ability by inservice training). In: Pädagogische Forschung, Heft 2, S. 49 ff.

— (1988a) Der junge Lehrer und seine Schüler (The young teacher and his pupils). Volk und Wissen Volkseigener Verlag, Berlin.

— (1988b) Der Pädagoge und seine Weiterbildung (The teacher and his inservice training). In: Jahrbuch 1988. Akademie der Pädagogischen Wissenschaften der DDR. Volk und Wissen Volkseigener Verlag, Berlin.

WAHLMANN, U. (1986) Die Rolle des Lehrers im Prozess der Ausbildung von Vorstellungen als Grundlage bei der Vermittlung und Aneignung soldier Kenntnisse über historische Sachverhalte im Heimatkundeunterricht bei Schülern unterer Klassen (The role of the teacher in the formation of notions as a basis of the giving and acquiring of solid knowledge of historic facts in local science for pupils of lower classes). Diss. A, Pädagogische Hochschule, Erfurt/Mühlhausen.

WOHLERT, W. (1972) Untersuchungen zu den wesentlichen Bedingungen für erfolgreiche Erarbeitung pädagogischer Lesungen — unter besonderer Berücksichtigung des Leitungsaspektes (Investigation of the relevant conditions for successful preparation of pedagogic lectures — under special observation of the guidance aspect). Diss. A, Humboldt-Universität, Berlin.

WÖLK, R. (1977) Uber Möglichkeiten der Erhöhung der Effektivität für die zukünftige sprachliche Weiterbildung der Russischlehrer durch eine wissenschaftlich begründete Stoffauswahl und über Wege zur Realisierung der Programminhalte (About possibilities for improving the efficiency of language training for teachers of the Russian language by a scientifically based selection of content and ways for the realization of programmes). Diss. A, Pädagogische Hochschule, Potsdam, 1977.

6

In-Service Training of Teachers: French Research

Francine Best and Monique Vial
(paper presented by Francine Vaniscote)
France

1. INTRODUCTION

There is a fairly little research into the in-service training of teachers in France. The two institutions mainly responsible for the further training of teachers, the "écoles normales" (training colleges) and "missions académiques" (regional education authority training units), tend to innovate, improve the structure of training sessions and rely on educational research rather than engage in self-evaluation or undertake research into the training they provide.

The INRP (National Educational Research Institute) directs and carries out research into teacher training. Mindful of the consequences for in-service training of the national goal of taking 80% of the young people in each age-group to level IV (the "baccalauréat"), the Institute devotes the bulk of the resources of one of its seven programme divisions to research in this field. If educational research in general and research into teacher training in particular are underrated in France, that is because they are overshadowed by the latent intellectual conflict between the traditional handing down of academic knowledge and personal vocational training of a pedagogical nature. Some academics and decision-makers continue to believe that a teacher mastering the contents of a subject will, for that very reason, be capable of teaching. Despite this obstacle, research is progressing. All the evidence suggests that in-service training (known as ''formation continue'' in France) has a very important role to play in the years ahead.

2. A DUAL TRAINING SYSTEM

Several studies carried out by Danielle Zay, a training college lecturer associated with the INRP, show a trend in the training colleges for primary teachers towards the formation of a kind of further training ''market'' in which supply and demand interact to enrich the subject-matter of training and adapt it to topical issues and practical necessities. Each year, in every French department, training college lecturers and directors offer a series of courses varying in length from one to six weeks. The teachers want these courses. They are entitled to a total of 36 weeks' in-service training throughout their 37 or 38 years of service.

Some sessions are held in the primary schools, if a group of teachers so request, with the assistance of the district inspector. Other sessions are held at the training college. University lecturers are invited to give talks on their research. Contrary to a mistaken opinion, which has been that of most decision-makers hitherto, co-operation between institutions does exist in training colleges, and particularly co-operation with academics specialising in education science or the teaching of a particular subject. This emerges from a study at the INRP by Bourdoncle and Zay.

The in-service training structure which the training colleges represent is, therefore, the subject of research, but continues to be disregarded by the decision-makers, who still only think in terms of the initial training of primary teachers and only allocate resources to the training colleges on that basis. For this reason, research concerning the training colleges also receives too little attention.

The training colleges have been organising in-service training for primary teachers since 1969, when the government decided to entrust them with this new task at the prompting of the Association of Training College Directors.

This training remains separate from the in-service training of lower and upper secondary teachers. The latter was entrusted to the regional education authority training units set up in 1982 following the report submitted by André de Peretti, then head of a research programme at the INRP, to the Education Minister, Alain

Savary. Here again, the pattern of further training depends on the subtle interplay between demand and the training provision set out each year in a training plan to achieve staff training goals. This is drawn up by the head of each unit, an academic who is attached to the chief education officer of each regional education authority or "academie" (each "académie" corresponds roughly to an economic region, comprising from three to six departments).

As in the case of primary teachers, the training sessions are held during working time. They usually last five days. The replacement of teachers attending such courses is a serious problem, more so than in the case of primary teachers, who, to some extent at least, are replaced by training college students.

Research was briefly carried out into the first regional education authority training plans to identify and assess secondary teachers' motivations with regard to further training. This research was directed by Raymond Bourdoncle at the INRP.

The separation of the two further training structures ("écoles normales" for primary teachers and "missions académiques" for secondary teachers) is the outstanding feature of in-service training in France. Furthermore, these training structures no doubt correspond to social and intellectual habits which have persisted in France since 1881 and the introduction of compulsory schooling. The sociology of education has shown, in another connection, that there are in effect two different professional cultures: that of primary teachers and that of secondary teachers (Isambert-Jamati, Revue Française de Pédadogie, INRP, 1985, No. 73, pages 57-65).

This duality of training is mentioned in the report by A. de Peretti and the studies of the INRP.

The few university courses set up by the university teacher training centres — there are some fairly active ones in Grenoble (IFM), Caen and Strasbourg — are no exception to this implicit rule. These centres are attended almost exclusively by secondary teachers, often to obtain a master's degree or diploma of further study, or even to write a thesis on education science. These courses are not an integral part of the regional education authority training system set up in 1982; the universities remain totally independent and free to set up teacher training centres or not.

This situation partly explains why the research deals sometimes with the training provided in the training colleges and sometimes with that which is organised, in some cases very judiciously and in association with research, as in Rennes or Lille, by the regional education authority training units (MAFPEN).

Another major phenomenon, brought out very clearly in the study by Danielle Zay, is the multitude of different rules which have governed the organisation of training colleges since 1969. These institutions went through no less than twelve different forms and training systems between 1979 and 1985.

Faced with such a profusion of structural changes, how is one to carry out relevant long-term research on evaluating the effects of initial training?

How is one to continue research into the ''ideal profile'' of the primary teacher (cf. research carried out by Marcel Postic), which could have served as a goal and provided criteria for evaluating the training given?

3. INDUCTION AS A PRIORITY AREA

In this state of affairs, the Director of the INRP urged researchers in 1983 to focus their research on the teacher's first steps in the profession. This decision was not only taken because of the impossibility or difficulty of evaluating the results of training arrangements which lasted for only two years, but also because at international conferences, organised in particular by the Council of Europe, this was the slant given to research into teacher training. Sociological and recruitment factors were changing the training situation and possible training goals so drastically that everyone — the Belgians, Germans and British alike — had given up evaluating training according to an abstract and theoretical profile of the perfect teacher, controlling the number and quality of relationships within the class and mastering teaching techniques. Induction is a particularly difficult experience which all teachers, primary and secondary, have to go through. What is more, it is a crucial point at which teachers can judge, criticise and evaluate their initial training and plan and promote the in-service training they need.

Provided these teachers are involved in an action-research programme, as in the case of the INRP research directed by Andre Louvet, we have here a situation and subject that are altogether positive from the research point of view.

100

Action-research of this kind has the advantage of being able to propose new forms of training. For example, it was found in the course of this research that the teachers needed regular meetings at which they exchanged information on the day-to-day difficulties encountered both in their schools and in their social and geographical environment. It is no longer a question of information or studies submitted by academics or training college lecturers, but of professional exchanges between peers, similar to further training arrangements for doctors (cf. so-called "BALINT" groups). This new form of training by no means rules out the existing courses and sessions: weeks of talks and debates on specific topics such as learning to read, primary school, the teaching of experimental science in the lower secondary school etc.

Research into the induction of teachers brings out a broad trend towards the increasing professionalisation of teaching. Teachers henceforth regard their occupation as a profession which has to be learnt, which requires them to master teaching skills as well as the subjects to be taught and to acquire pedagogical as well as academic knowledge.

Another sign of this increasing professionalisation is that some universities, such as the University of Saint-Etienne, have set up ''pre-professionalisation'' courses for students studying for the training college entrance examination.

Nevertheless, the concept of in-service training as that of learning continuously over a long period has not yet achieved the recognition it deserves in this trend towards increasing professionalisation.

4. SUMMER COURSES

There is, however, one area of training which has been advocating the idea of permanent, life- or career-long education for a very long time (since 1945, if not since 1936), with short intensive courses on a residential basis. This is the training of holiday or leisure centre workers by state-approved training institutions, the main ones being the centres for training in Active Education Methods, the League for permanent education and the Federation of state educational and holiday organisations.

It is in this framework that research is being carried out on the effectiveness of one-week courses and alternate periods of training and fieldwork. The reasons why we are mentioning this research and these innovative training methods here is that many teachers (in particular, all training college students, for whom these courses were for a long time compulsory) received training from these institutions in addition to their university and vocational training. It was in this framework, therefore, that teachers encountered the theory and practice of in-service training. The practical research carried out by these bodies (in particular the centres for training in active education methods) is aimed at innovation in the form and content of training: it is research which sets out to produce proposals rather than to evaluate.

Lastly, the year 1982 saw the introduction of "universités d'été" (summer courses). The initiative for these courses, which, like those just mentioned, are held during the teachers' holidays, may come from educational movements such as those mentioned above, or from regional education authority training units, or from a ministerial department, or from the INRP, or from a group within the inspectorate.

For a period of a week, the teachers (whose numbers vary from 30 to 100) receive advanced information from academics and researchers and discuss such topical educational issues as education in human rights, literature for children and young people, digitised images and their uses, telecommunications and education etc. These summer courses, which are half-way between the colloquy and the seminar form, are highly successful and undermine the view that teachers are unwilling to undergo training during their holidays.

5. PROBLEMS AND FORWARD PLANNING

In-service training as it is experienced by French teachers is a voluntary activity. What was a positive quality at the time of its introduction (1969 and 1982) is in the process of becoming a defect. The teachers who enrol for training and choose the subjects or courses are the innovators, those who are deeply committed to their professional life. For this reason, the availability of in-service training is purely theoretical in the case of the great majority of French teachers who do not avail themselves of this possibility. Yet some aspects, such as the initial stages in the first year of primary school or guidance throughout lower secondary education, would seem to call for compulsory training.

The lack of planning of further training curricula leads to the same negative result. Not everything is centralised in France, far from it. However paradoxical this may seem, the extreme decentralisation of training (each regional education authority, and each department in the case of primary education, has its own further training policy and plan) precludes planning which would take account of the proportion of teachers trained or not trained in a particular region and of the most important educational issues identified at national level by the INRP or other bodies. What about the international issues? Without central government planning of training open to teachers from several countries, one fails to see, in the present situation, how systematic changes on specific topics would be possible.

These comments show the need for forward-looking research which would prove useful to decision-makers by enabling them to identify subjects for in-service training according to their degree of urgency. The "computing for all" plan should be reviewed, with much clearer goals and better planning than in its initial form (in 1985). This is only one example. Other subjects, such as education in human rights, are equally important.

Lastly, it seems desirable, after the research already carried out, to consolidate and improve the structure of the link between research and further training. In the Rennes regional education authority, training/research groups meet regularly, carry out action-research into specific educational topics (especially in the field of teaching methods and theory), organise information days for their colleagues and thus become trainers themselves. Indeed, the sole purpose of this research is to improve training. In the light of experience, the region's chief education officer and the head of the training unit have realised that training through research and participation in research is the best in-service training formula.

With better planning of further training, one could experiment more widely with this training model, linking research closely and continuously to training, and not leave it confined to the Rennes regional education authority. One could even — and the association of some 4,000 teachers with the INRP would make this possible — make the research-training link an appropriate subject of research.

But for such research to be developed, decision-makers must share the belief that in-service training is of paramount importance at a time when there is a consensus on the priority that should be given to education.

Part 2
National and Individual Reports

7

How can we Transform the Methods Used by Serving Teachers?

M Crahay
Belgium

1. PREAMBLE

A number of experiments have been carried out in the last ten years in the field of in-service training of teachers. Some have met with success, if only partially; others have failed. How can we explain the success of some attempts and the failure of others? We may feel, like Kurt Levin, that "there is nothing more practical than a good theory", that is to say, a conceptual framework which suggests a valid explanation for what works and what does not work.

Our aim is not to devise a general theory of in-service training but — more modestly — to analyse the experiments carried out at Liège University's Experimental Teaching Laboratory over the last 15 years in order to see how it is possible to change teachers' methods in a way that will last.

2. REALISING THE CONSTRAINTS OF THE SITUATION AND LEARNING HOW TO DEAL WITH THEM

The technique of micro-teaching and the behavioural approaches which follow in its wake mean focusing on behaviour patterns considered to be undesirable and asking the teacher, by the use of video or other means, to modify that behaviour. This approach was tried and then abandoned by the researchers in the Experimental Teaching Laboratory, when an experiment conducted by Martin (1970) showed clearly that this training procedure did not bring about lasting changes in teaching practice.

In the first stage of the experiment the researcher observed and analysed a teachers' methods during several lessons. From this initial observation it emerged that the teacher — like many others — usually provided "poor quality" feedback ("That's right", "That's wrong"). The researcher-instructor informed the teacher of this and explained that, according to the most recent learning theories, it was important to provide more specific feedback of the type "That's right because ..." or "That's wrong because ...". He invited the teacher to do some reading on the educational value of more specific feedback. The teacher reacted very positively to his reading. Everything seemed to indicate that the teacher had been aroused to an important new awareness. Action was decided upon: the teacher undertook to change the kind of feedback he used with the pupils. The researcher-instructor would assess the changes in the teacher's methods and keep him informed of the progress of the experiment.

At the end of the experiment the teacher and the researchers suffered a great disappointment. The teacher had indeed succeeded in changing the kind of feedback he used during the early lessons of the second stage of the experiment, but very quickly had lapsed back into his old habits.

Let us conclude first of all from this experiment that "where there's a will there is not always a way". We shall then try to understand more completely why this failure occurred.

More detailed re-examination of this experiment showed that the teacher succeeded in giving a great many specific types of feedback during short phases of his lesson. These phases were characterised by questions which stimulated the advanced intellectual processes. On the other hand, during other, more frequent, parts of the lesson, the teacher asked simple restitution-type questions. The pupils gave short replies to these questions, to which the teacher reacted with a simple feedback.

108

This repeat analysis reveals — as demonstrated by a number of American research projects — how patterns of teaching behaviour are interdependent and that in order to change teachers' feedback their way of asking questions has to be changed according to the following clarification:

Restitution question ———— short replies ———— simple feedback

Questions stimulating ———— lengthier replies ———— specific feeback
higher cognitive processes

This clarification does not, however, end the questioning process. For it is not enough to ask questions stimulating the higher cognitive processes in order to be able to give more specific feedback and, if the teacher mentioned above acted from time to time in that way, why is it not possible to extend this method of interacting with the pupils to the whole of the lesson?

This is by no means an innocuous question. It reflects the failure experienced by a good number of researchers — particularly Americans — who have tried to modify teachers' questioning patterns. Three researchers, Kounin (1970) and Doyle and Ponder (1975), have produced a series of works providing explanations of this resistance to change. According to Kounin the teachers who succeed best in organising pupil participation are those who have a good "momentum", that is to say those who manage to ensure a steady flow of classroom activities and to avoid sudden changes as well as excessive interruptions and delays. Doyle and Ponder have continued this work and have shown that questions presenting some difficulty may disturb the class atmosphere. A question stimulating the higher cognitive processes inevitably requires more time for thought than a simple restitution question: the reply itself will be longer and more complex. Some pupils may become confused in their explanations: fellow-pupils are tempted to intervene and make their contribution. Others who have found the solution quickly become bored while waiting for the slower ones and at times even make fun of the laborious nature of some of their fellow-pupils' replies. When teachers are asked about their decision-making processes by means of stimulated recall (a technique whereby the teacher is asked to remember outstanding parts of the lesson and the decisions he took, the teacher being helped by seeing a video of the lesson), we discover that they experience this kind of event as a critical moment in the life of the class: the success of the activity is at stake. The most common reaction is to take a short-cut, either by finding a "reliable pupil" who will give the right answer clearly or by giving the answer oneself. In both cases the aim is to enable the lesson to proceed.

These considerations may seem far removed from questions of in-service training focused on teachers' methods. Yet they bring us to the very centre of the discussion. In particular, the work of Kounin and Doyle and Ponder takes the debate beyond the notion of resistance to change. That notion certainly has some advantages: instructors and researchers can explain their lack of success by putting it down to the conservatism of the teachers. This is an easy reaction but it seems over-hasty. The originality of the work of Kounin and Doyle and Ponder is that they have demonstrated how the atmosphere of a class or the success of a particular activity is the result of a delicate balance and that by suggesting certain innovations the instructor or the researcher destroys this balance. In other words, he introduces confusion more so than a change for the better.

Should we conclude from all this that we should refrain from suggesting new ways of stimulating a class and — to take up again the example given above — accept that most teachers will be satisfied with simple restitution questions? Certainly not. It leads us instead to affirm that a specific change in teaching practice presuppose reshaping the whole teaching situation and, from that viewpoint, the teacher's preparation work for the activity is of crucial importance. We are now working along those lines both with trainee teachers and with experienced teachers. Our job consists in helping them to prepare lesson plans, ways of regrouping pupils and the teaching aids which will enable them to adopt a different style of teaching, while at the same time retaining pupil participation.

It is not simply a matter of restoring lesson preparation to a place of honour. More precisely, that facet of teaching which the British call preactive teaching must be given its full dimension. In our view, the teacher in the teaching situation has difficulty in thinking about what he does. The classroom is an environment where events follow one another at a furious rate. There are even times when a number of important events occur simultaneously; as Jackson (1969) points out, in the classroom the teacher is under constant pressure to act swiftly and decisively. Taking a few moments to think about the most appropriate course of action is frequently — according to Huberman (1986) in particular — the thing not to do because such a pause for thought may create further difficulties for him.

To repeat a forceful phrase from Doyle and Ponder, "In the classroom it is not the teacher who controls the situation but the situation which controls the teacher". On the other hand, when preparing an activity the teacher has complete freedom to think about his or her actions or, more precisely, to arrange a teaching situation which will lead to the use of one behavioural pattern rather than another.

This view of the job is not immediately accepted by the teachers. For them it means radically changing the way they look at themselves, the way they see themselves. They have to abandon the idea that their actions are the direct reflection of their will or personality. They have to accept that they must regard their power of decision as limited by the constraints of the teaching situation and that their behaviour in the classroom is as much — if not more so — controlled by the situation than by their free will.

It is the very basis of their psychological concepts — what are now called implicit personality theories — which have to be radically transformed.

3. ACTION IN TERMS OF IMPLICIT THEORIES OF TEACHING AND TEACHER PERSONALITY

A technological approach to continuous training leads to the notion that it is important to provide teachers with tools which are immediately usable. This notion has now become self-evident. It is not, however, enough.

A number of research programmes carried out in the Experimental Teaching Laboratory and designed to persuade teachers to practise formative education (in particular the PREDIC research programme) have fallen victim to this illusion (which also lies in wait for innovation in information technology). The principle behind this research was simple, namely that it was not enough to recommend to teachers a mastery of their subject and the use of formative evaluation, nor to explain in detail the work and the writings of Bloom; teachers should be provided with instruments which are ready for use and easily applied, particularly in regard to formative tests.

In reality, teachers use those tests which have a direct bearing on the subjects included in the syllabus but, frequently, the tests fulfil the function previously served by questions asked by the teacher; they are used in particular to assess pupils and hardly at all to identify learning problems. In other words, formative tests are used in a normative manner, which is paradoxical and which rarely leads to corrective measures being taken.

How can we explain this "perversion" of formative tests?

Once again it seems that the concept of "implicit personality theory" must be invoked. For if teachers divert formative tests away from their original purpose (to identify the learning problems of some pupils in order that they can overcome them and achieve equal success) it is because deep down they do not associate themselves fully with that aim. When pressed to say what they really think, many say "That's all Utopian" or "Let's be serious: some pupils are gifted and others are not and teaching cannot remedy nature".

How can we change the implicit personality theories which teachers carry around with them?

The APER experiment conducted by a number of researchers in the Experimental Teaching Laboratory (A Grisay, R De Bal, V De Landsheere and M Detheux) opens up some new approaches in this context. The ultimate objective of the research is to reduce academic failure in Belgian schools. (However, at present the operation is confined to the state system in the province of Liège). To attain that objective the teachers' methods, and in particular their assessment methods, must be completely changed.

Rather than recommending certain approaches the researchers in the APER team decided to provoke the teachers taking part in the experiment into rethinking their behaviour or even knocking them off balance. They proceeded to set pupils in all classes at a given level (for example, those in second year primary school) the same attainment test. Simultaneously they gathered together the examinations set by the teachers and the results obtained by pupils in these examinations. Lastly, they asked the teachers to order a series of learning objectives for each teaching level.

Once this information is assembled a comparison procedure, or what Huberman calls data triangulation, can be organised.

When the pupil's results on the attainment test are compared with those they obtained in the examination set by their teacher a whole range of phenomena emerge — for example, that:

— the marks of the pupils in the class are more widely spread in the examination than in the attainment test. This phenomenon, which is repeated in practically all the classes, reflects the tendency of teachers to overestimate the differences between the pupils in their class;
— pupils whom a teacher wants to repeat the year would, with the same attainment level, be near the top if they were in another class.

An analysis of the content of the examination papers taken by the pupils shows, in the case of nearly all the teachers, that they systematically go beyond the syllabus (for example, two-thirds of the questions set in second year primary school French examinations are concerned with grammar whereas this subject is not in the syllabus; only a preliminary oral grounding is prescribed).

Moreover, when the list of examination questions which they and their colleagues set is communicated to the teachers the very great majority manifest their amazement at the extent to which they went beyond the syllabus, and a relative unanimity emerges on the "acceptability" of the examination content at a given academic level.

Experience shows that this comparative procedure leads to reconsideration, whereupon the teachers want an approach which will enable them to make their methods more coherent. This approach inevitably involves updating and thinking about their implicit theories on personality and teaching. Many teachers ultimately realise that if they examine their pupils on subjects dealt with in the following year it is because they want to ensure that there will be a spread in the examination marks.

Why do they try to produce this kind of spread? Is it justified? .... All these questions arise almost naturally from the comparison of data and lead on to what is at the heart of the educative activity, namely the intuitive theories of teachers.

4. CREATING INTERACTIVE NETWORKS AMONG TEACHERS

It would nevertheless be wrong to restrict in-service training to the psychological or individual level. A teacher wanting to change his methods is frequently subject to a series of pressures from those who try to keep him within "the norms", by having him continue to use methods conventionally regarded as "normal".

In the course of various research programmes carried out by the Experimental Teaching Laboratory we have collected some concrete examples where a teacher's attempts to innovate have been thwarted by his colleagues, his headmaster, or in some cases even by the parents of children at the school.

On the other hand, it was noticed that where the innovation was maintained beyond the in-service activity undertaken by the researchers a social dynamism was created around the innovating teachers. This interactive dynamism which takes over, as it were, from the training situation to which it was introduced by an external agent appears as an essential condition for the stability of innovations. We might quote in connection with in-service training what Bronfenbrenner observed in connection with remedial education: "It is as if the individual is unable to interiorise immediate changes for any length of time; whereas an interactive system (parent-child, in the case of remedial education) enables him to do so".

This observation leads us to look at in-service training no longer simply in terms of individual learning but also in terms of social interaction. We must insist on this because the danger of misunderstanding is great. What is needed is to combine an approach centred on the cognitive change of the individual with an approach oriented towards the interactive, but not to substitute one for the other.

LITERATURE

BLOOM, B.S. (1979) *Caractéristiques individuelles et apprentissages scolaires,* Brussels: Labor.

DOYLE, W. & PONDER, G.A. (1975) "Classroom Ecology: some concern about a neglected dimension of research on teaching". *Contemporary Education, Vol. XLVI,* 3, Spring, pp 183-188.

GRISAY, A. (1984) "Les mirages de l'évaluation scolaire. Rendement en français notes et échecs a l'école primaire". *Revue* of the Directorate General of Organisation of Studies, May, 29-42, and June, 9-23.

GRISAY, A. (1986) The APER research project: First results and prospects, University of Liège, Experimental Teaching Laboratory, APER document No. 8.

HUBERMAN, A.M. (1983) S'évaluer pour s'illusionner? Promesses et écueil de l'évaluation adaptative/interactive des innovations scolaires, Neuchâtel, IRDP/R: 83.08, Publication of the GCR/SSRE.

HUBERMAN, A.M. (1986) "Repertoires, recettes et vies de la classe: comment les enseignants utilisent l'information". In M. Crahay & D'Lafontaine (Eds), *L'Art et la Science de l'Enseignement*, Brussels: Labor.

JACKSON, P.W. (1968) *Life in Classrooms,* New York: Holt, Rinehart and Winston.

KOUNIN, J. (1970) *Discipline and Group Management in Classrooms*, New York: Holt, Rinehart and Winston.

MARTIN, J.M. (1970) *Attempt to control change in the teaching behaviour of a primary school teacher*, University of Liège, Unpublished *Licence* dissertation.

8

Milieu and Leadership in the School - a Norwegian INSET Project Without Goal Attainment

Kari Johansen and Arild Tjeldvoll
Norway

1. INTRODUCTION

"Milieu and leadership in the school" (MOLIS) was a nationwide project under the auspices of the Norwegian Council for Primary and Lower Secondary Education in co-operation with regional school governors, starting in 1981. The purpose of the project, which over a 6-year period cost about 6 million kroner (approximately £640,000), was to carry out school development and train school leaders.

On the conclusion of the MOLIS project on 1st July 1987, the Norwegian Council for Primary and Lower Secondary Education gave the Institute for Educational Research at the University of Oslo the task of summing up the project.

2. WHAT DID WE LOOK INTO?

The aim of the investigation was to examine the influence of the MOLIS project on Norwegian primary and junior secondary schools in regard to school development and the training of school leaders. In our opinion the effect on schools would largely depend on the central planning and organisation of the MOLIS project. In addition, we assumed that the results of the project would be associated with the ways in which the Education Officers conducted the MOLIS courses. The plan, organisation and implementation of the project had therefore also to be included in the evaluation.

Our professional starting-point is that school development and school-leader training are instruments in the creation of a better school for the pupils. The attributes of a better school are to be found in the aims of the National Curriculum (Monsterplanen). And, since evidence of school development should above all be manifested in the pupils, it is our view that the teacher, as the one who takes the lessons every day and who is responsible for taking care of the pupils, is the most important person when it comes to inservice preparation.

3. HOW WE SET UP THE INVESTIGATION

In order to obtain information on the implementation and effects of MOLIS we interviewed altogether 60 persons, consisting of three regional school governors, the staffs of three local education offices and the staffs of six schools. In addition, we carried out a questionnaire inquiry at every regional education office in Norway, from which we attempted to map the ways in which the regional school governors implemented the MOLIS courses in their region. In the interview investigation we gave priority to depth over breadth, so that this material does not provide a basis for generalised conclusions on a national scale. The questionnaire inquiry included all the regional education authorities, which makes it possible to say something about general tendencies as well as variation between the regions.

4. OUR FINDINGS

(1) The MOLIS program was, on the whole, carried out conscientiously in the various regions. All the same, there was considerable variation in the quality of the courses. Only a few regions attempted to co-ordinate MOLIS with the rest of the further training courses in the region. However, it looks as though this changed a little when the revised National Curriculum came into force in 1986. There were also only a few regions with a sufficiently critical attitude towards the program to take compensatory action when they discovered its weak points.

(2) We found few effects in the form of school-leader training. The results we were able to register concerned attitudes and reactions in the sphere of personal relations. Some people considered that their awareness in regard to their pedagogical and administrative work was heightened, but we have very few definite examples of this.

(3) Our material does not provide a basis for saying that the goal of school development was achieved. To start with, there were few activities which included the whole school. The common activities we were able to register had to do with particular changes in the organisation of the school day, or the physical environment in and out of doors. Examples of this were the introduction of a "midday break arrangement" and "tidying up the teachers' library". These activities seem to have been chosen more or less at random, according to what the school found problematic at a given time, and were therefore not necessarily connected with the National Curriculum. Some teachers considered that they had changed their own attitudes and forms of communication, which in their opinion may have had an effect on the pupils. A few teachers reported one or two changes in their teaching, usually that they had started to use methods such as "involvement education" or "an integrated day". These teachers did not know whether such changes were due to MOLIS or other courses they had attended on those subjects. So it looks as though MOLIS reached the level of teachers and pupils only to a minimal extent.

5. WHY WAS THERE NO SCHOOL DEVELOPMENT?

We shall try to explain these results by calling attention to certain features of the MOLIS program's plan, organisation and implementation.

117

The aims of MOLIS were concentrated on interpersonal relations, and could therefore relate to the aims of the National Curriculum only as regards attitudes. We have no sound basis for supporting the supposition of MOLIS that a good environment automatically leads to better learning for the pupils. Neither do those effects that we were able to register imply that a good staff atmosphere automatically leads to teachers' becoming better at teaching. It seems, therefore, that the training aims of MOLIS for school leaders and teachers were too limited to comply completely with the aims of the National Curriculum.

The content of the MOLIS program, with its environmental and interpersonal emphasis, was relevant only in a limited sense to the goals of the National Curriculum and the teachers' tasks. Exercises in co-operation and training in communication were the dominant themes, so that the content had the character of various methods and techniques for regulating social interaction. The methods of work were often based on personal practice and personal experiences, with relatively less emphasis on the transmission of knowledge. From our recording of effects, it was doubtful whether the courses provided learning in the sense that the participants could convey or use knowledge for the benefit of the school. In our opinion, knowledge of education (in the meaning of completeness and of critical understanding of upbringing, teaching and education) is a pre-condition of teachers' evaluation of their own teaching and of their practical involvement in taking care of the pupils. An adequate knowledge of education is also necessary in order to be able to evaluate teaching and to analyse the weak and strong sides of one's own work.

Several of our informants called attention to the above-mentioned weak points in the program. One of them said that MOLIS meant "learning the techniques of co-operation without knowing what to co-operate about". Another used the description: "MOLIS greases the machinery without knowing what the machine is supposed to do". These pronouncements reveal the lack of emphasis laid by MOLIS on both the aims of the school and its subject matter.

The strategy of MOLIS was mainly aimed at training leaders who were to follow up the training by initiating school development and carrying it out together with their staffs. The lack of results from the project may mean that the school leaders had not internalised the knowledge acquired at the courses sufficiently to be able to be "teachers of the staff" back at school. When the leader has nothing to give, no further training will result for the teachers. This is especially unsatisfactory because for several years MOLIS was funded by the district educational advisory services, whose job is to provide for the further training and guidance of both school leaders and teachers. That MOLIS focused on leaders may in addition have had the unfortunate effect of consolidating the school's hierarchical structure, thereby obstructing democracy and co-determination. MOLIS provided skills in using techniques to influence people, which can be used as a hidden means of control. The leader could personally select what to convey back to school and so exert greater influence on the choice of subject for development work. For school development, the teaching staff also require training. It doesn't look as though the leadership strategy of MOLIS was capable of fulfilling such a demand.

The MOLIS program did not have continuous and systematic evaluation built in, which meant that the project leaders had difficulty in telling whether the aims of school development and leadership training were being fulfilled during the process. Lack of evaluation also made it difficult to see the project's strong and weak points and to revise it accordingly.

In our opinion weaknesses in organisation contributed to the project's having so little influence. It was particularly serious that MOLIS co-operated to such a slight extent with professional experts from colleges and universities; neither did it make use of professional advisory bodies such as the Norwegian Council for Primary and Lower Secondary Education. This lack of co-operation may have been due to the notion that academic bodies had little relevance for the school system. The separation of MOLIS activities from the rest of further training would also appear disadvantageous, both in regard to resources and professionally. The project leaders had a great deal of freedom, both of action and in the delegation of authority. In our view the powers of the central authorities (the Ministry of Education and the Norwegian Council for Primary and Lower Secondary Education) to exert control were correspondingly weakened.

6. CONCLUSIONS

(1) If the aim is to initiate school development in order to better implement the National Curriculum for the benefit of the pupils, we consider that the strategy must be based on training and development within the schools. This implies the theoretical and practical inservice training of whole teaching staffs.

(2) The selection of content and methods of work must make internalisation of knowledge and skills possible, so that teachers and leaders alike become qualified for their practical work. The qualifications must include a broad

119

knowledge of Education. Teachers must be given proficiency in relation to the task of the school in society, the pupils' varying backgrounds and the set framework of the school (its laws, regulations and finance, the organisation of the physical environment in and out of doors and the allocation of time and human resources).

(3) An inservice training program for the initiation of school development must have built in the continuous and systematic evaluation of the program, its organisation and courses. Evaluation must include every level of the educational system.

MOLIS came as a natural consequence of three of the main tendencies of the 70s:
— the emphasis placed by educational policies on the social environment,
— political subscription to the ideas of democratisation and co-determination,
— the attention paid by trade and industry to the importance of leaders of organisations, and the development of a new style of leadership.

From this perspective MOLIS was in tune with the times. It is only now possible to pass judgement on the effects of the measures taken on the basis of these currents of thought.

In this light the MOLIS project has contributed valuable experience on which to build when future models of inservice training programs for the educational sector are to be designed.

LITERATURE

Detailed information in English on MOLIS is contained in:

JOHANSEN, K. & TJELDVOLL, A. School Development and Educational Competence. A Summary of the Final Evaluation of "Milieu and Leadership in the School". Institute for Educational Research, University of Oslo, 1988, 21 p.

9

In-Service Teacher Education in Berlin (West)

W Fest
Federal Republic of Germany

Instead of an institute for in-service, Berlin operates a network for professional development. The Berlin Ministry of Education utilizes the resources in Berlin, West Germany and Europe to meet teacher requests for in-service activities and to stimulate professional development in general.

Part of the programme is offered by the Educational Centre, the Central Institute for the Training of Teaching Attitudes and the Documentation of Instruction, and the Media Centre. Whereas these three institutions are administrative bodies of the Ministry, there are various other institutions that co-operate with the state authorities in sponsoring and conducting in-service courses. Among the partners of the Ministry are business, universities, professional organisations, unions, foreign cultural services etc.

The Ministry provides funding, scheduling and promotion for in- service. Other organisations provide the programmes which are developed and conducted in accord with the school supervisors. On the above basis a programme which consists of some 400 courses per semester, and in which more than 7,000 teachers can participate, is offered twice a year. Statistically, every teacher out of a teaching body of 18,000 can take part in an in-service activity every one-and-a-half years.

Attendance at in-service courses is on a voluntary basis, because teachers are required by the law to improve their education but are not obliged to attend certain courses. Thus, any programme organised for them must meet their needs and interests.

Traditionally, teachers' demands were measured on the basis of trends in participation, reports of supervisors and requests by professional organisations or individual teachers.

To attain more reliable results about teachers' interests an inquiry has been carried out recently.

At first, a pilot study concentrated on the acceptance of in-service courses offered by the Free University of Berlin. This survey provided the methodological instruments (questionnaires and SPSS evaluation) for a larger inquiry into the effectiveness of INSET in Berlin.

In the winter of 1986-87 the teaching staff of 24 representative schools were questioned with the aid of a questionnaire consisting of 15 questions. This inquiry was supported by a number of interviews with teachers. The major finding was that most teachers in Berlin are motivated to take part in in-servicing in order to update their academic achievements, to obtain precise, comprehensive information on subject-matter, to increase their own competence or to widen their general education. The main interest is in refresher courses which extend their knowledge of their teaching subjects. Secondly, there is a demand for didactic and methodological aids. Additional motives include a wish for exchanging experience with other colleagues and the ambition to acquire a formal qualification. The intensity of these motives varies according to the teacher's age, gender, type of school and teaching subject. Such differences have then to be taken into account for the planning of new courses directed at teachers in a particular type of school. Likewise, the correlation between teaching subject and interest has been examined, because a great number of courses are directed at teachers of a common subject or a group of similar subjects such as foreign languages.

Another issue is the organisation of courses. Here the aspects of application for leave of absence and their regulation by the district authorities was examined. Only a minority of teachers were not granted leave when applying for it, but teachers would prefer a reduction of their teaching obligation for in-service purposes. Such reductions of the teaching load are so far limited to university courses preparing for certification in a new subject. Despite problems arising from obtaining leave, most teachers pleaded for compact seminars over two or three days instead of weekly sessions in the afternoon or evening. Very few were willing to spend part of their vacations on in-service, but weekends are accepted to a certain extent.

Response was positive to special forms like excursions and inservice courses for the needs of a particular school. Among the institutions offering in-service courses, the universities were ranked first in popularity, followed by the Education Centre, foreign cultural services, teachers' professional associations and business. As for lecturers, although priorities were less clear, university and school teachers were preferred to teacher trainers or lecturers from other spheres.

To test the effectiveness of the present in-service programme, teachers were asked how they assessed the likelihood of the subject-matter of in-service courses transferring into practical teaching and, furthermore, how their expectations were met in the courses attended. The results were not spectacular but confirmed some of the assumptions of the organisers: transfer into instruction is mostly indirect and expectations were predominantly, or at least partly, fulfilled.

The inquiry described above will serve as a basis for the more systematic pursuit of in-service activities. It will help to develop new courses in fields hitherto neglected and also help to improve the organisational framework for in-service. The data provide information that is relevant for teacher trainers and all individuals and institutions engaged in in-service.

Future research is envisaged on special subjects like vocational training, sports and the teaching of migrants. At present, another inquiry in progress at the Free University of Berlin is examining the response of teachers to courses for professional development.

LITERATURE

Ausschuss für Lehrerbildung (1985) Forderungen an eine qualifizierte Lehrerfortbildung, Berlin.
FEST, W. (1985) Neue Perspektiven in der Lehrerfortbildung. In: *Brennpunkt Lehrerbildung*, Heft 1, S. 17-18.
FEST, W.; KRETSCHMER, H.; STARY, J. & WILSDORF-SELKA, E. (1987) 5 Semester Lehrerfortbildung an der FU. In: *Brennpunkt Lehrerbildung*, Heft 6, S. 38-44.

FRECH, H., MANDELARTZ, M. (1985) Mehr Radikalitat tut Not. In: *Berliner Lehrerzeitung* Nr. 7/8, S. 23-25.

HARNISCHFEGER, W. (1986) Qualifikation nicht dem Zufall überlassen. In: *Berliner Lehrerzeitung*, Nr. 6, S. 11-13.

HARNISCHFEGER, W. (1988) Senat zufrieden — wir nicht. In: *Berliner Lehrerzeitung*, Nr. 5, S. 28-29.

KRETSCHMER, H. (1985) Fort — und Weiterbildung für Lehrer Konzepte und Erfahrungen. In: *Brennpunkt Lehrerbildung*, Nr. 1, S. 10-15.

Der Senator für Schulwesen, Berufsausbildung und Sport (1987) Berichte über die Umfrage zur Lehrerfort — und weiterbildung, Berlin.

10

The Efficiency of Long Term Supplementary Training

The Bulgarian UNESCO Commission

1. INTRODUCTION

Scientific and technological progress have led to increasing demands on the training of young people, who are today taught at school three basic types of knowledge: that which is already confirmed, that which is hypothetical and that which is prognosticative. The faster hypotheses and prognoses are confirmed, the greater the need in society for the permanent upgrading of teaching personnel. If we all have to engage in life-long learning, this is even more important for teachers.

This is a basic principle for any system of inservice training for teachers. We have always taken the greatest interest in the extent to which intellectual effort, work, materials, financial investment and resources have contributed to this end. We have always evaluated whether the results were worth the time spent for this purpose. In this respect, the system of upgrading teaching staff is based on the cybernetic theory of Norbert Winer — that of management through feedback. Although any system of inservice training can be improved if the methods and means of its evaluation are reliable, the better the evaluation and estimation of its efficiency, the better the training system will be, with higher quality and better results.

2. DEFINITION OF TERMS

Since the theory of education has not yet an agreed system of terms, one should always specify the basic terms used in any theoretical, practical or research work. What follows are our basic terms with their definitions.

2.1 General Terms

System of inservice training of teachers and heads of educational institutions. This, as a sub-system of national education, forms an integral part of the nationwide system for the training of all working people. The purpose of the system is to provide continuous and permanent upgrading of the teachers throughout their active professional, social and cultural life. The system's structure comprises the aims and tasks of the system, the educational groups included in it, the teachers and educational staff engaged in the training, the assistants and professors in higher education institutions, the contents of the professional qualification, the types and forms of inservice training and the financing and creation of its material and technical basis.

Levels of inservice courses. These are the different levels for the organisation of inservice courses: school, town, region, nation.

Types of courses. Depending on their duration, these are long-term (from six months to two or three years) and short-term (up to six months). In general, their purpose is the dissemination of new knowledge, that of specialisation in different fields or requalification when necessary.

2.2 Terms connected with estimating the efficiency of the upgrading process.

Efficiency. The positive results of the work, as compared with the effort expended and the necessary resources for a given period of time.

Effectiveness. A process is effective if it is successful and achieves good results.

Quality. The properties of the training process which determine its ability to satisfy its intended requirements.

In this study the terms *efficiency* and *effectiveness* are used as synonyms and attention will be paid first of all to the efficiency of the form of training (or qualification) and its activities.

3. ESTIMATION OF EFFICIENCY

According to the different levels of training activity, different systems for estimating the training of teachers and educational staff are used. Further, we shall consider the so-called continuous forms of training which are characteristic of the national institutions charged with these functions. They include training courses or fellowships of six months, one year, two years, and three or four years duration.

Generally, these forms of training are provided by the institutions of higher education in our country. Within some of them, the University of Sofia, for example, there are specialised institutes as autonomous faculties. Actually, these are the institutions which are directly connected with the systematic study of the efficiency of the training process of teachers and educational staff.

The analysis of efficiency takes place in three stages.

The first stage is at the level of the course or the fellowship. At the beginning of each course tests are held to assess the professionalism of the participants. At the end of the course tests are again used to assess the new training level of the participants — what knowledge they have acquired, what qualities they have retained, what conclusions for their own professional activity they have made, how they make prognoses, how they organise the progress of their pedagogical work, what innovations and new technologies they want to put into practice and what kind of new research they plan to undertake.

The second stage is that of an analysis of similar forms of training undertaken every six months at the level of the faculty or department. In this case the achievements of the trainees are regarded as the criterion of the development and improvement of the training itself — what kinds of new subjects and problems should be studied in the lecture courses, at the seminars and laboratory exercises, what kinds of new training technologies must be put into practice or spread more widely, what additional research work it is necessary to undertake and so on.

The third stage is the collection of materials for the practical work of the teachers in school after having finished the training course. For example, how many and what kind of software programmes (from the number of programmes they developed during training in the institute) do they use in their teaching; whether there are any changes in relationship between the teacher and the

127

pupils, the headmaster and the teachers or the headmaster and the pupils; what kind of studies the teacher or the headmaster has organised or put into practice; what new publications he has succeeded in bringing out in the educational press; what personal contribution he has made to the general intellectual development of his pupils, to the rise of the social prestige of the school and the teaching staff in general. The collection of facts like these should be systematised and analysed annually and discussed thoroughly at a special meeting of the Faculty Council at the institute at the end of each academic year. The decisions of the Faculty Council should form the basis for the development and improvement of the training process for the next year.

The system of analysing the results of the fellowship trainees is relatively autonomous. Each trainee works according to a programme, prepared beforehand and approved by the Faculty Council, which sets out the necessary studies and experiments. The results of every part of this programme are reported periodically and discussed thoroughly at the departmental meetings. Depending on the concrete results of the trainee's work, his tutor may recommend his participation in seminars, symposia and conferences at a national or international level. Such a meeting or conference gathering of specialists in his field can evaluate his results and suggest new ideas for the further development of his scientific research programme. This means that the trainee during his studies already takes an active part in scientific research in his field and makes his modest contribution. After the end of his research programme and the preparation of his thesis, his papers may be discussed publicly, when he defends his thesis and hypotheses. The efficiency in this case is determined by the public estimation of the trainee's work and its practical implementation in a concrete teaching situation.

4. CRITERIA, INDICES AND INSTRUMENTS

The system of criteria, indices and instruments for measuring the efficiency of the educational process is usually as follows:

4.1 Estimation of the efficiency of the training process at the institute where the training takes place

Criteria	Indices	Instruments
1. Preliminary qualifications of teachers who are to be trained	1. Need for training	Conversations
	2. Motives for further training	Answers to questions
	3. Aptitude for self-training	Different kinds of tests
2. Changes in the professional qualification at the end of the supplementary training	1. Increase and durability of the knowledge	Solving of problems, incidents, etc
	2. Confirmed convictions	Practical Problems
	3. New forms and methods of work acquired during the training	Different kinds of tests

4.2 Professional activity of the teachers and heads of educational institutions at their place of work

Criteria	Indices	Instruments
1. State of the educational (pedagogical) process	1. Thoroughness and solidity of the knowledge of the pupils	Evaluation at three levels: top, medium and low
	2. Utilisation of technical means of education	Observation of the training, process and extra-curricular work
	3. State of activity of the pupils	
	4. Relative share of the original work of the pupils	
	5. Utilisation of different forms and methods by the teacher	Different kinds of tests and so on
	6. Relationships between the teachers and the pupils, etc.	

5. RESEARCH PROJECTS IN BULGARIA

In the People's Republic of Bulgaria the efficiency of the training of teaching staff and heads of educational institutions is given permanent attention as a problem which is neither isolated nor episodic. Efficiency is an integral part of the whole training activity in all its aspects. Its consideration and analysis is obligatory in all the institutions and organisations that are responsible for the training of educational staff. The estimation of its efficiency is obligatory for every teacher who has taken part in the training process. Besides, most of the institutions of higher education where inservice training is held systematically organise specialised theoretical and practical studies aimed at the improvement of methods, criteria and indices, as well as the techniques of applied research. These studies can generally be divided into two main groups.

5.1 First: studies of a fundamental scientific character
The main problems which are subject to study and experiment are related in most cases to:

- the clear definition of the purpose and the tasks of the training process and the adequate determination of the ways, forms and means which may indicate to what extent they are achieved in every single case;
- specification of the social, human and professional criteria and indices which are characteristic of the quality and efficiency of the training process;
- elaboration of research mechanisms, techniques and procedures which are able to neutralise as much as possible any subjective approach in the evaluation so that it can be really relevant, objective and reliable.

5.2 Second: concrete studies of the efficiency of the training process for given subjects and training areas.
For example, the efficiency of the form of training specially for English language teachers is different from the form of training for teachers of physics and chemistry as well as for teachers of painting. That is why every single case needs elaboration of its strictly specific instruments and specific research techniques.

6. CONCLUSIONS

In the People's Republic of Bulgaria there exists a large-scale system of supplementary training of teachers and heads of educational institutions all over the country. The analysis of the quality and the efficiency of the training process is an integral part of this system. We can share with pleasure the experience that we already have with all countries and institutes which take an interest in it.

The People's Republic of Bulgaria offers fellowships to specialists from all over the world who wish to undertake studies and experiments of their own in our country under the specific supervision of Bulgarian specialists.

The People's Republic of Bulgaria can offer qualified specialists for research work and experiments in the field of the organisation of training projects (including the estimation of the efficiency of the training process) in all interested countries.

Bulgarian specialists in the training of teachers and educational staff are interested in the organisation of joint scientific projects and the publication of comparative analyses on the efficiency of the training process.

These proposals can be realised with the help of UNESCO or on the basis of bilateral or multilateral conventions that may be planned and agreed within the framework of international co-operation.

LITERATURE

1. LAKEURESKY, Al. (1984) One of the projects for a system of evaluation of the efficiency of the training process. *Improving the inservice training of teachers.* Volume I, Sofia, pp 79-85.
2. SIMEONOV, Il. (1984) The necessity of a better technology for the upgrading process. *Improving the inservice training of teachers.* Volume I, Sofia, pp 90-97.
3. NESTOROV, P. (1984) The supplementary training of teachers. Basic trends in the socialist organisation of pedagogical work. *Qualifications activity of the commissions of practical research,* Sofia, 1984, pp 7-13.
4. NESTOROV, P. (1984) Possible criteria for the evaluation of the qualification of teachers. *Improving the inservice training of teachers.* Volume I, Sofia, pp 85-89.

5. YOLOVA, Ts. (1983) Improvement of the purpose and end characteristics of the upgrading process of teachers of vocational polytechnical training. *Problems in the intensification of teacher training*, Sofia, pp 248-257.

6. BRUTOVA, T. (1983) Improvement of the study of the Bulgarian language by establishing the professional level of the teachers. *Problems in the intensification of teacher training*, Sofia, pp 173-183.

7. VULKOVA, St, IVANOVA, V. et al. (1983) Innovation of the training process on the basis of the reconstruction of the pedagogical work in classes I-III. *Problems in the intensification of teacher training*, Sofia, pp 132-162.

11
INSET as a
Realisation of the Idea
of Permanent Education

Stanislaw Kaczor
Poland

1. INTRODUCTION

One of the aims of the Conference is to review current research and analyse the results of completed research into the quality and effectiveness of teachers' work. The results obtained will serve as a basis for the achievement of the next aim, which is to suggest topics for future research in the light of recent trends, needs and social and individual demand in this field. The main theme of the Conference is concerned specifically with the effectiveness of in-service teacher training.

The purpose of this paper is to set out some particularly complex issues which require clarification so that the results obtained can meet practical requirements.

2. TERMINOLOGICAL AND METHODOLOGICAL DIFFICULTIES

Although the term "effectiveness" is frequently used in education, a precise determination of its meaning and content always raises difficulties, especially from the practical point of view. To say that effectiveness is a relationship between the result and the means employed to achieve that result is not a sufficient answer because further questions arise, for example, concerning the evaluation of the time, energy or money expended in relation to the actual output.

It therefore seems advisable to carry out further research into the various aspects of effectiveness. In Poland, for example, the concept of effectiveness should be studied in relation to the following "contexts": (1) capacity, (2) output, (3) skills, (4) the functional aspect, (5) the communicative aspect and (6) moral values (see, for example, Holstein-Beck, 1987). Attention should also be drawn in this connection to the concept of "ecological" effectiveness, which, as such, comes before moral and ethical values.

Given the contexts enumerated above, the research in question can to some extent be useful for determining the content of the concept of effectiveness of in-service teacher training. Surveys conducted in Polish schools on the role and functions of the teacher show that the professional skills most appreciated by young people are competence, effectiveness and then, among the ethical and social values, fairness.

There is another question which strikes us as being important: the specific character of the effects of educational action. Many of those responsible for education policy expect immediate effects in this field, whereas, on the contrary, the most beneficial effects are those obtained in the long term. This is inevitable because, in education, all processes of change take place slowly, and often their effects are not noticeable for many years. The same applies to the results of teachers' work, which also become perceptible in the long term, after a relatively long period of time (cf. "Educational goals", UNESCO, Paris 1981).

3. IN-SERVICE TRAINING AND THE TEACHER'S FUNCTIONS

The teacher's functions stem from those of the school and other educational institutions. We identify five main functions, which are subject to change:

(1)   the educative function
(2)   the didactic function
(3)   the social and protective function
(4)   the investigative function
(5)   the innovative function

As a result of surveys carried out for six years in succession in vocational schools with the aim of ascertaining young people's opinions and attitudes, we are already in a position to state the problems which have to be taken into account in the process of in-service teacher training in the various forms of organisation of the education system.

Improvement is clearly an obligation from which no one is exempt. The forms of organisation stem from teachers' respective teaching methods and experience. The aims and contents of curricula must meet the needs and requirements of those concerned. This applies not only to teachers but above all to pupils.

To improve the educative function, an attempt must be made to understand more clearly how the individual operates within the group. It is necessary not only to individualise the teaching and learning process, but also to discover each pupil's possibilities. Conditions and situations conducive to individual development must be created. It is significant that, for Polish pupils in vocational schools, the most important thing is that the teachers should show respect for their personal dignity. The process of in-service training should therefore take account of the psychological principles underlying education, which make it possible to control the group's activity while respecting the individual's needs and rights. The problem of active pupil participation also falls within the scope of the educational function. Pupils should have more decision-making power with regard to the choice of subjects, the mode of operation of youth organisations and teachers' working methods.

Improvement of the didactic function involves above all combating the old view that education is the sole source of knowledge. Curricula are too full and we are still seeing a situation in which, instead of studying and understanding, pupils merely assimilate the contents of curricula. They have to learn fast but they also forget.

In accordance with the idea of permanent education, school learning is merely a stage in the learning of life. The sources of information are currently very varied and constantly increasing in number, the broadcasting of television programmes by satellite being one example. Where, then, are the difficulties with regard to access to information and the improvement of teaching methods? Teachers seem to have difficulty in selecting essential information. In this particular instance we share the view of other specialists, namely that the modern teacher acts above all as a guide in the world of knowledge and moral values: he is more a counsellor than a source of knowledge.

The personal example given by the teacher himself in his work and attitude plays and, it seems, will continue in future to play an important role in the performance of the educational function.

The improvement of the social and protective function is related to the needs resulting from young people's circumstances. Material difficulties, family conflicts, social questions, the organisation of leisure activities etc. - all these are problems to which the teacher should always be receptive while showing his commitment and determination to help his pupils. Teachers should possess interdisciplinary knowledge which will enable them, among other things, to intervene in often very complicated situations relating to their pupils' personal difficulties.

Everyone, including teachers, wants to succeed at work. Systematic research, which should be encouraged among teachers, serves to identify the source of difficulties, thus making it possible to find effective ways of remedying them. According to the results of our surveys, teachers have a great need for an easy means of checking the results of teaching and learning. Research methods must be improved, as must the creation of the motivation necessary for the development of this type of activity. The conclusion may be as follows: improvement of the teacher's professional skills must be combined with the development of his or her general scientific culture. This is a condition which will enable scientific progress to be used for the benefit of the teacher and school.

Lastly, let us move on to the development and improvement of the innovatory function. For various reasons, the obligation of continually improving working methods does not concern all teachers. In this field, one very often finds activities which are more on the lines of mere changes than of improvements or innovations. For this reason, especially in vocational schools, any innovation in teaching methods must be introduced after a prior study of trends in the development of techniques, in the pattern of work and especially in the occupations reflecting the division of labour in the various sectors of the national economy. The teacher must therefore have the essential knowledge as regards jobs and as regards scientific and technological progress in general (the positive and negative aspects of the development of scientific and technological civilisation).

Further training programmes for teachers are drawn up in the light of the results of studies carried out in this field. The suggestions above are an illustration of this. Another very important problem is the preparation of training staff. Candidates should have a high standard of education and numerous abilities, especially as regards the application of theory to practice.

LITERATURE

GRZYBEK, H. (1984) *L'éfficacité du perfectionnement des enseignants:* a study of six training courses. Czestochowa, pp 233.
HOLSTEIN-BECK, W. (1987) *Les essais sur le travail.* Warsaw, pp 249.
KACZOR, S. (in press) "L'enquête sur les opinions et les attitudes des jeunes dans les écoles professionnelles (1982-1987)". Warsaw, *La Pédagogie du Travail No. 13.*
WIATROWSKI, Z. (1982) *L'enseignant de l'école professionnelle.* Warsaw, pp 185.
WIECZOREK, T. (1981) *La formation et le perfectionnement des enseignants pour écoles d'agriculture.* Warsaw, pp 203.

12

The Effectiveness of INSET in Hungary

Péter Szebenyi
Hungary

1. INTRODUCTION

In 1985 the Ministry of Education passed a new decree for the further education of teachers which created more favourable conditions for the modernisation of INSET. The question remained, however, as to what should or could be the course of this development. The research begun in 1985 under the auspices of the National Institute for Education covered the following issues: (1) information on teachers' opinions about their own further education was collected; (2) the forms and content of INSET within and outside the various public educational institutions were surveyed; (3) the most important background documents on the history of teachers' in-service training were collected; (4) the main international trends were studied; (5) a developmental experiment was started, one of the tasks of which was to examine the possibilities of modernising INSET (Bognar, 1986). We have made use of points (1) and (5), particularly as regards the effectiveness of INSET, its results and its shortcomings. Further data can be found in the overall statistics of the Institute of the Ministry of Education for Science Engineering and Information Processing.

2. QUANTITY AND EFFECTIVENESS

It is reasonable to assume that participation rates are, to some extent, related to the effectiveness of in-service training since in Hungary there has not been compulsory further education for teachers, nor is it still compulsory, for the past thirty years. Participation and effectiveness are related in the sense that more teachers attend the useful and interesting courses, and also in the sense that suitable forms of INSET create the possibility for attendance. Undoubtedly, other factors also influence attendance, such as, for instance, how overworked the teachers are within and outside school, how much they are morally and financially motivated to participate in further education and whether they are formally or informally pressed to attend in-service training courses. Whatever the reasons for attendance or non-attendance, the numbers attending, or more precisely the ratio of attendance to the total number of teachers, is an important indicator of the effectiveness of INSET.

The first of the studies listed above was implemented in 1985. It involved a national sample of 1,000 teachers, representative by type of school (8-grade primary and 4-grade secondary), settlement, sex and age. The figures showed that between 1980 and 1985 91 per cent of the teachers attended some sort of in-service training course. Moreover, 42.1 per cent took part in such occasions three or more times. In 1985, the year of the study, 53,165 teachers, or 27.8 per cent of the teaching force, took part in INSET.

Are these figures high or low? There are neighbouring countries where INSET is compulsory every five years. In 1985, it seemed likely that INSET every five years would be realised in Hungary too, though central directives were not issued. The situation also seemed favourable in comparison with other professions. In the early 80s, 18 per cent of the graduated population took part in some sort of further education course. This included 15% of professional medical workers, 11% of the technical intelligentsia, 8% of agricultural workers, 2% of economists and 33% of teachers.

The picture is not so bright, however, if we look at the trends in Table 2.1.

Table 2.1. Percentage of teachers taking part in INSET.

Year	1980	1981	1982	1983	1984	1985	1986
%	49.2	43.6	39.7	32.2	32.7	27.8	18.6

The table shows that the number of teachers participating in INSET has markedly decreased. Moreover, certain anomalies can also be discovered if we study the composition of the participants. For example, the figures show that there are unjustifiably large differences in attendance between particular groups of teachers (Table 2.2).

Table 2.2. Teachers attending INSET courses as a percentage of the total numbers of teachers in 1986.

Type of school	Percentage attendance
Kindergarten (3-6 year olds)	9.3
8-grade primary school (6-14 year olds)	23.8
Day-time home at primary schools (afternoon occupations)	12.9
4-grade secondary school (14-18 year olds)	30.7
3-grade vocational school (14-17 year olds)	10.2

Further data obtained in the representative study of 1985 showed that teachers from the 1-4 grade primary schools were also under-represented.

These proportions are difficult to justify. It is true that kindergarten teachers and lower elementary school teachers (grades 1-4) are more difficult to find substitutes for than, say, secondary school teachers. But this is not so in the case of vocational school teachers. Nor can it be said that those groups of teachers with lower attendance figures need less further education. It is remarkable that 23.8 per cent of the teachers interviewed said that they could not attend courses because their applications were refused, while the same figure was 34.7 per cent in the case of elementary school teachers. Since this means that every third applicant was turned down, we must therefore conclude that there is a touch of elitism in the present system of Hungarian INSET, given that more attention is paid to teachers who work in schools preparing children for higher education, certainly as regards the form of INSET. As for the content of INSET, 64 per cent of the 4-grade secondary (grammar school) teachers and 70.7 per cent of the 3-grade vocational school teachers claimed that they were in at least one in-service training occasion that they judged to be useless.

The age-division of teachers participating in INSET cannot be said to be satisfactory, given that the following table represents the situation.

Table 2.3. Age participation rates (as percentages).

Age	All Teachers	Teachers taking part in INSET
29 year olds and younger	32	23
30 year olds and older	68	77

The 1985 survey showed that teachers with less than five years teaching took less part in INSET courses and received less information about further education. In short, they are one of the most neglected groups of teachers in this respect in Hungary. Some people say that it is natural that this is so because these teachers are fresh from the universities. But in reality higher education can hardly undertake the practical training and socialization of beginning teachers. This task should be solved, as in other countries, within the framework of INSET. We must also remember that since higher educational institutions do not undertake as much as they could of this work, the effectiveness of education depends, to a large extent, on the organisation of further education for beginner teachers.

3. POSSIBILITIES AND DEMANDS

The afore-mentioned decree of 1985 introduced several types and forms of INSET: extension courses at universities and colleges, panel seminars, professional conferences, forums, summer universities, target courses in preparation for the implementation of new curricula, complex (theoretical and practical) seminars, subject pedagogy and technology of instruction courses, special courses for day-time (afternoon) teachers, form-masters and school librarians, training courses for principals, participation in professional competitions, experiments and studies, guided self-education etc. These and other forms exist and take place. In the representative survey of 1985 the teachers mentioned the following forms of INSET in which they had participated in the previous five years: (1) subject courses, 91.0% of the teachers questioned; (2) special courses for form-masters, day-time (afternoon) teachers etc., 31.4%; (3) ideological courses, 16.6%; (4) cultural courses, 7.6%; (5) youth activist courses, 7.5%.

The following types of INSET presentation were identified: (1) lectures, 34.6%, (2) courses for teachers' panels, 24.3%, (3) show lessons, 19.8%, (4) complex seminars, 18.2%; (5) conferences, 10.4%; (6) small-group training sessions, 6.4%; (7) summer universities, 4.7%; (8) debating circles, 4.5%; (9) open universities, 2.0%; (10) creative camps, 1.2%.

Although these types and forms of further education can only be effective if they are able to meet the teachers' demands, it was not so according to the 1985 survey. Further education training was dominated by courses and course-like gatherings in which lectures were delivered. The interviews indicated, how-ever, that not only those teachers living a good way off from centres but also those who possess the necessary skills, but who suffer from lack of time, would welcome the currently almost non-existent possibilities of guided self-education. These opinions coincide with the answers given to the question "What prevented you from participating in one of the interesting forms of INSET?" The reasons given were as follows: (1) responsibilities at school, 33.7%; (2) home or financial difficulties, 25.8%; (3) application refused, 21.9%; (4) poor transport facilities, 1.6%.

The teachers interviewed also made it clear that they would prefer training which combined lectures, debates, and opportunities for the exchange of experiences. It is also worth quoting the answers to the question "What is the aim of INSET?".

The aims of INSET	Percentage response
Learning new methods	60.2
Acquisition of new special knowledge	47.3
Asking for educational-methodological assistance	41.8
Inspiration for self-education	40.6
Brushing up special knowledge	31.8
Exchange of experiences	16.5
To study the new curriculum	11.1

While the demand for "learning new methods" was mentioned most frequently, there were big differences between particular groups of teachers in this respect. Mostly day-time (afternoon) teachers (70.8%) and teachers graduating from Lower Primary School Teachers' Training Colleges (65.8%) placed this de-mand on the top of their list, while teachers with a university degree needed it the least (52.4%). Conversely, teachers working in grammar schools (58.2%)

and those with a university degree (57.3%) placed first the acquisition of specialist knowledge, whereas the corresponding percentages in the case of teachers graduating from Lower Primary School Teachers' Training Colleges and teachers working in grade 1-4 primary schools were 34.6 and 37.2 respectively. If we recall that the central educational government prefers the demands of teachers graduating from universities by assuring them one-year courses at universities (by providing absence from school for 120 lessons per year and granting a pay-rise for teachers with the best results) and if we know that the acquisition of specialist knowledge is dominant in these courses then we can only conclude once again that the available forms of INSET favour the demands of grammar school teachers at the expense of the remainder. This situation detracts from the effectiveness of INSET from the outset. The effectiveness of this system is also questioned by the fact that about half of the state-guaranteed 5,000 prescribed places for teachers who can participate in the one-year intensive university courses usually remain vacant.

Today it is more and more difficult to get teachers and schools to take part in INSET. It is therefore all the more important to make their actual demands agree with the real possibilities. This is, however, only one side of the issue, since it is not at all certain that the subjective demands of teachers and the objective demands of children, their parents and the country will always coincide. We consequently need to find ways of inspiring teachers to participate in further education training that will help to raise the effectiveness of the educational-instructional process. The fifth research study mentioned in the Introduction was an attempt to achieve this goal.

4. SCHOOL-BASED AS ACTION-BASED INSET

Altogether, 30 primary schools of an industrial town (Kazincbarcika) of 40,000 inhabitants and with a similar number of inhabitants in its neighbourhood were involved in a research study in the school-year of 1985-86. The goal of the study was to reorganise the school-inspectorate system and the renewal of the traditional system of INSET was also made part of this reorganisation. We managed to develop the local, school-based INSET with partial success. However, in the primary schools, where the need for INSET was greatest, the teaching staff were unable to plan and organise school-based INSET. At this point we started organising inter-school panels with the participation of teachers from the teaching staffs of the village schools. Only a few of these proved to be viable and improvement had to be achieved by other means. Firstly, the consultants themselves arranged open days and delivered show lessons instead of sitting in on teachers' lessons. Teachers in great numbers visited these lessons and even joined in training of a more theoretical character, but as passive participants. They became more active when teams of consultants together with teachers' panels and inter-school panels began to study, in a given field of education, the minimum objectives determined by central curricula. Even the collecting of instruments required a lot of reading and learning of new things. After identifying the various problems, the majority of panels got down to obtaining diverse educational programs, adapting new methods, criticising and improving the central curriculum and, in this way, realising action-based development.

The main experience of this initiative, which is still on-going, is that the special problems of INSET can only be solved within the complete framework of the program for the development of public education. In Hungary, the new Educational Law of 1985 strengthened the independence of schools and teachers' panels. If it is connected with systematic and objective control of the results and with the planned establishment of the examination system, school-based development will surely gain ground and involve a strengthening of the demands for INSET and its restructuring. Therefore we would like to develop gradually a flexible, colourful, servicing system of INSET that could meet both existing and new demands.

LITERATURE

BOGNAR, T. (1986) *Teachers' Views on the Systems of INSET*. OPI, Budapest.
GONCZOL, E. & SZEBENYI, P. (1981) *Development Trends in Teachers' Further Education*. OPI, Budapest.

Appendix I

List of Participants

Fürstl. Studienrat (Chairman), Dr Josef WOLF, Leiter des Schulamtes, Hotel Adler, FL — 9490 VADUZ

Professor Dr Wolfgang MITTER (Rapporteur), Deutsches Inst. f. Intern. Pädagogische Forschung, Schloss-Strasse 29, Postfach 90 02 80, D — 6000 FRANKFURT AM MAIN

Doc. JUDr Svatopluk PETRÁČEK (Keynote Speaker), Director of the European Information Centre for Further Education of Teachers, Charles University, Kaprova 14 CS — 11000 PRAHA 1

Professor Michael R ERAUT (Lecturer), Chairman of Education and Professor of Continuing and Professional Education, University of Sussex, EDB Falmer, GB — BRIGHTON BN1 9RG

Monique VIAL (excused)

Francine VANISCOTTE (Lecturer), Professeur d'Ecole Normale, Chargée d'études sur la formation au Centre International d'Etudes Pédagogiques de Sèvres, Chercheur associée a l'INRP, INRP DP 4, 29, rue d'Ulm, F — 75230 PARIS Cedex 05

Professor Dr Helmut STOLZ (Lecturer), Direktor des Zentralinstituts für Weiterbildung der Lehrer und Erzieher DDR — 1721 LUDWIGSFELDE

Professor Viktor G ONUSHKIN (Lecturer), Academician, Director of the Research Institute for Adult Education, USSR Academy of Pedagogical Sciences, Nab. Kutuzova 8, SU 191 187 — LENINGRAD/USSR

Dr Rudolf Batliner (Lecturer), Pädagogischer Mitarbeiter, Schulamt, Hotel Adler, FL — 9490 VADUZ

II. DELEGATES

ALBANIA: (excused)

AUSTRIA: Hofrat Dr Hildegard PFANNER, Landesschulinspektorin, Landesschulrat f. Vlbg. Landhaus, A — 6900 BREGENZ

BELGIUM: Professor Pol DUPONT, Président de l'Institut des Sciences de l'Education de l'Université de Mons, 139, rue du Commerce, B — 7370 ELOUGES

Professor J HEENE, Directeur, Seminaire et laboratoire de didactique, Président du Conseil Interfacultaire des Enseignants (aggrégation), Université de l'état, 2 Henri Dunantlaan, B — 9000 GAND

BULGARIA: Todor ANGUELOV, General Secretary of the Higher Educational Council, Ministry of Culture, Science and Education, 18, Stambomiisky blvd, BG — 1040 SOFIA

Vera DESPOTOVA, Bulgarian National Commission for UNESCO, 96b rakovsky str. PO Box 386, BG — 1040 SOFIA

BYELORUSSIAN SSR: (excused)

CANADA: Dr G WHITE, Associate Dean, Faculty of Education, Queen's University, CND — KINGSTON, Ontario K7L 3N6

CYPRUS: Dr Panayiotis PERSIANIS, Director of the Pedagogical Institute, 11, Othonos, Akropolis, CY-NICOSIA 141

CZECHOSLOVAKIA: Doc. JUDr Svatopluk PETRÁČEK, CSc., Director of the European Information Centre for Further Education of Teachers, Charles University, Kaprova 14, ČS — 11000 PRAHA 1

PhDr Hana PROCHÁZKOVÁ, European Information Centre for Further Education of Teachers, Charles University, Kaprova 14, ČS — 11000 PRAHA 1

PhDr Marie ČERNÁ, CSc. European Information Centre for Further Education of Teachers, Charles University, Kaprova 14, ČS — 11000 PRAHA 1

PhDr ZUZANA KOLLÁRIKOVÁ, Director, Central Institute for the Education of Teachers, Budysinska 3, ČS — BRATISLAVA

Doc. Dr KAREL TMEJ, Director, Central Institute for the Education of Educational Personnel, Myslikova 7, ČS — 11000 PRAHA 1

DENMARK: Borge PRIEN, Danmarks Paedagogiske Institut, Hermodsgade 28, DK — 2200 KØBENHAVN NV

FINLAND: Dr Sauli TAKALA, Institute for Educational Research, University of Jyväskylä, Seminaarinkatu 15, SF — 401000 JYVÄSKYLÄ

FRANCE: Pierre DELORME (excused)

Michel BOULET, Directeur de l'Institut National de Recherches et d'Applications Pédagogiques (INRAP), 2 rue des Champs-Prévois, F — 21000 DIJON

Francine VANISCOTTE, Professeur d'Ecole Normale, Chargée d'études sur la formation au Centre International d'Etudes Pédagogiques de Sèvres, Chercheur associée à l'INRP, INRP DP4, 29, rue d'Ulm, F — 75230, PARIS Cedex 05

FEDERAL REPUBLIC OF GERMANY: Dr Wolfgang BÜNDER, Institut für die Pädagogik der Naturwissenschaften (IPN), an der Universität Kiel, Olshausenstrasse 62, D — 2300 KIEL

Dr Wilfried Bernhard FEST, beim Senator für Schulwesen, Bredtschneider-strasse 5-8, D — 1000 BERLIN 19

Dr Hans SIMONIS, Direktor des Staatlichen Instituts für Lehrerfort- und weiterbildung des Landes Rheinland-Pfalz, Butenschönstrasse 1, D — 6720 SPEYER

GERMAN DEMOCRATIC REPUBLIC: Professor Dr Helmut STOLZ, Direktor des Zentralinstituts für Weiterbildung der Lehrer und Erzieher, DDR — 1721 LUDWIGSFELDE

Dr Manfred HAAK, Wissenschaftlicher Mitarbeiter, Zentralinstitut für Weiter-bildung der Lehrer und Erzieher, DDR — 1721 LUDWIGSFELDE

149

GREECE: Christos FRANGOS, Professor of Education, President of the Department of Education at the University of Thessaloniki, Director of the Educational Research Centre and In-service Training (EDURIT), Department of Education, University of Thessaloniki, GR — THESSALONIKI

George MARKOU, University of Athens, Department: Philosophy — Pedagogik — Psychology, Section: Pedagogic, Gaziasstr. 1-3, ILISIA 15771, GR — ATHENS

HOLY SEE: Rév. Père Gilbert CAFFIN, 5, rue Trubner, F — 67000 STRASBOURG

HUNGARY: Professor Dr Miklos SZABOLCSI, Director General, National Institute of Education, Gorkij fasor 17/21, H — 1071 BUDAPEST

Dr Péter SZEBENYI, Director, Centre for Orszagos Pedagogiai Intezet, Gorkij fasor 17/21, H — 1071 BUDAPEST

ICELAND: Professor Sigridur VALGEIRSDOTTIR, Director of the Institute of Educational Research, V/Laufasveg, ISL — 101 REYKJAVIK

IRELAND: Dr Thomas KELLAGHAN, Director of the Educational Research Centre, St. Patrick's College, IRL — DUBLIN 9

ISRAEL: Professor Michael CHEN, Head, School of Education, Tel-Aviv University, Ramat-Aviv 69978, TEL-AVIV, Israel

ITALY: Dr Paolo DALESSANDRO, Ispettore centrale, Ministero della Pubblica Istruzione Ufficio degli Studi e Programmazione, Via Ippolito Nievo 35, I — 00153 ROMA

LIECHTENSTEIN: Fürstlicher Studienrat, Dr Josef WOLF, Leiter des Schulamtes, Hotel Adler, FL — 9490 VADUZ

Dr Rudolf BATLINER, Pädagogischer Mitarbeiter, Schulamt, Hotel Adler, FL — 9490 VADUZ

Dr Bruno WETTSTEIN, Pädagogischer Mitarbeiter, Schulamt, Hotel Adler, FL — 9490 VADUZ

LUXEMBOURG: Georges WIRTGEN, Directeur de L'Institut Supérieur d'Etudes et de Recherches pédagogiques, BP2, route de Diekirch, L — 7201 WALFERDANGE

MALTA: Dr Kenneth WAIN, Senior Lecturer, Faculty of Education, University of Malta, TAL-QROQQ, MSIDA, Malta

NETHERLANDS: Dr Johannes LODEWIJKS GLC, Managing Director, Institute for Educational Research in the Netherlands (SVO), Sweelinckplein 14, NL — 2517 GK THE HAGUE

NORWAY: Agnar SLETTELAND, Rector, Bergen Teacher Training College, Landassvingen 15, N — 5030 LANDAS

Professor Arild TJELDVOLL, Associated Professor/Director, Educational Research Institute, University of Oslo, PO Box 1092 Blindern, N — 1317 OSLO 3

POLAND: Professor Tadeusz LEWOWICKI, Director of the Pedagogical Research Institute, ul. Gorczewsks 8, PL — 01-180 WARSZAWA

Professor Stanislaw KACZOR, Director of the Institute of Vocational Training ul. Mokotowska 16/20, PL — 00-561 WARSZAWA

PORTUGAL: Professor Manuel F PATRICIO, Président de l'Institut d'Innovation Educative, Trav. Terrass Sant'Ana, 15, P — 1200 LISBOA

Maria DO CARMO CLIMACO, Directrice du Service du Bureau d'Etudes et de Planification, Av. Miguel Bombarda, 20, P — 1093 LISBOA Codex

ROMANIA: (excused)

SAN MARINO: Carla NICOLINI, Preside, Scuola Secondaria Superiore Statale, Contrada Santa Croce, RSM — 47031 CITTÀ DI SAN MARINO

Silvia BERTI, Universitary, Via della Tana 121, RSM — 47031 CITTA DI SAN MARINO

SPAIN: Angel RIVIERE, Director of CIDE, Centro Nacional de Investigación y Documentación Educativa Ciudad Universitaria s/n, E — 28040 MADRID

SWEDEN: Dr Inger MARKLUND, Research Director, National Board of Education, Department of Planning, S — 106 42 STOCKHOLM

SWITZERLAND: Dr Willy JEANNERET, Expert fédéral de l'enseignement commercial, Directeur du Centre interregional perfectionnement, Pres 35, CH — 2720 TRAMELAN

Hans-Rudolf LANKER, Leiter der Zentralstelle für Lehrerfortbildung Kirchstrasse 70, CH — 3089 BERN

Jacques-André TSCHOUMY, Directeur de l'Institut romand de recherche et de documentation pédagogiques (IRDP) Fbg. de l'Hôpital 43, CH — 2000 NEUCHÂTEL

TURKEY: (excused)

UNITED KINGDOM: Professor Guy NEAVE, Professor of Comparative Education, DICE, University of London, Institute of Education, 20 Bedford Way, GB — LONDON WC1H 0AL

Dr John Alexander WILSON, Director, The Northern Ireland Council for Educational Research, The Queen's University of Belfast, 52, Malone Road, GB — BELFAST BT9 5BS

Professor Michael R. ERAUT, Chairman of Education and Professor of Continuing and Professional Education, University of Sussex, EDB, Falmer, GB — BRIGHTON BN1 9RG

Dr Seamus HEGARTY, Deputy Director, The National Foundation for Educational Research, The Mere, Upton Park, GB — SLOUGH, SL1 2DQ

UKRAINIAN SSR: Dr Yuri Petrovich GUDZ, Vice-Rector on Instruction, Kiev Gorki State Teacher Training College, 9, Pirogov Street, SU — 25 20 30 KIEV/USSR

Dr A.SIROTENKO, Institute for Scientific Research, KIEV/USSR

USSR: Milhail MIKHNO, Chief of Educational Section, USSR Commission for UNESCO, Av. Kalinine 9, MOSCOW/USSR

Professor Viktor G. ONUSHKIN, Academician, Director of the Research Institute for Adult Education, Academy of Pedagogical Sciences, Kutuzova 8, SU — 191 187 — LENINGRAD/USSR

YUGOSLAVIA: Dr Darko ŠTRAJN, Director, Pedagoski Institut, Gerbiceva 62, YU — 6111 LJUBLJANA

III. PARLIAMENTARY ASSEMBLY OF THE COUNCIL OF EUROPE

Sénateur Rafael ROMAN (Commission de la Culture et de l'Education), Paseo Maritimo 1, E — 11010 CADIZ

Felix HASSLER, Vice-Président de la Commission des relations avec les pays européens non membres, Oberbühl 94, FL — 9487 GAMPRIN

IV. OBSERVERS

WORLD CONFEDERATION OF ORGANISATIONS OF THE TEACHING PROFESSION (WCOTP)
Mrs Mai TRA-BACH, WCOTP, 5 avenue du Moulin, CH — 1110 MORGES

OECD
Alan WAGNER, Principal Administrator, Centre for Educational Research and Innovation, OECD, 2 rue Andre Pascal, F — 75775 PARIS CEDEX 16

ICET (INTERNATIONAL COUNCIL ON EDUCATION FOR TEACHING) ATEE WORKING GROUP 12 (THE PROFESSIONAL DEVELOPMENT OF TEACHERS)
Dr A.Michael VAN DER DUSSEN, RIJNSBURGERWEG 146, NL — 2333 AJ LEIDEN

INTERNATIONAL LABOUR OFFICE (ILO)
(excused)

INTERNATIONAL ASSOCIATION FOR THE EVALUATION OF EDUCATIONAL ACHIEVEMENT (ILEA)
Dr Inger MARKLUND, Head of Division, National Board of Education, S — 106 42 STOCKHOLM

EUROPEAN TRADE UNION CONFEDERATION
(excused)

COMMISSION OF THE EUROPEAN COMMUNITIES
(excused)

V. ORGANISERS

UNESCO/UNESCO INSTITUTE FOR EDUCATION (HAMBURG)
Etienne BRUNSWIC, Director, Division of Educational Sciences, Content
and Methods of Education, UNESCO, 7 Place de Fontenoy, F — 75700
PARIS

Dr Ravindra H. DAVE, Director, UNESCO Institute for Education, Feld-
brunnenstrasse 58, D — 2000 HAMBURG 13

Dr Hans-Wolf RISSOM, Regional Adviser, Division of Educational
Sciences, Content and Methods of Education, UNESCO, 7, Place de
Fontenoy, F — 75700 PARIS

COUNCIL OF EUROPE
Maitland STOBART, Deputy Director of Education, Culture and Sport,
BP 431 R6, F — 67006 STRASBOURG Cedex

Dr Michael VORBECK, Head of the Section for Educational Research and
Documentation, Council of Europe, BP 431 R6, F — 67006 STRASBOURG
Cedex

Sylviane WEYL, Section for Educational Research and Documentation,
Council of Europe, BP 431 R6, F — 67006 STRASBOURG Cedex

Heather HENDRY, Directorate of Education, Culture and Sport, BP 431 R6,
F. — 67006 STRASBOURG Cedex

*EUROPEAN INFORMATION CENTRE FOR FURTHER EDUCATION
OF TEACHERS (EIC-FET)*
Doc. JuDr Svatopluk PETRÁČEK, CSc., Director EIC-FET, Charles
University, Kaprova 14, ČS — 11000 PRAHA 1

PhDr Marie ČERNÁ, CSc., EIF-FET, Charles University, Kaprova 14, ČS — 11000 PRAHA 1

PhDr Hana PROCHÁZKOVÁ, EIC-FET, Charles University, Kaprova 14, ČS — 11000 PRAHA 1

LIECHTENSTEIN
Fürstlicher Studienrat, Dr Josef WOLF, Leiter des Schulamtes, Hotel Adler, FL — 9490 VADUZ

Dr Bruno WETTSTEIN, Pädagogischer Mitarbeiter, Schulamt, Hotel Adler, FL — 9490 VADUZ

Rosmarie CIPOLLA, Sekretärin, Schulamt, Hotel Adler, FL — 9490 VADUZ

VI. INTERPRETERS

Natacha AGAPIEFF, 16, chemin de la Tourelle, CH — 1209 GENEVE

Irina ROOS, 120, chemin des Mollies, CH — 1293 Bellevue-GENEVE

Bettine HUERNI, 2 rue des Confessions, Apt. 32, CH — 1203 GENEVE

Helga McGREW-WALTER, 8 chemin de la Béraille, CH — 1226 Thomex, GENEVE

Jacques VICHNIAC, 18, rue de Beaumont, CH — 1206 GENEVE

Micheline KARAM-CLEUSIX, 21, chemin de la Montagne, CH — 1224 Chenes-Bougeries, GENEVE

Francis-Jan DITTRICH, 30, rue de Vermont, CH — 1202 GENEVE

Nancy DARGEL, 49, ave d'Aire, CH — 1203 GENEVE

André BERNHARD, Bureau des Interprètes, Conseil de l'Europe, BP 436 R6 F — 67006 STRASBOURG Cedex

Appendix II

List of Conference Papers

1. KEYNOTE AND COMMISSIONED PAPERS

Keynote: "Meeting the challenges of the nineties: trends in in-service education and training (INSET) of educational personnel" by Dr Svatopluk PETRÁČEK, Czechoslovakia (doc. DECS/Rech (88) 32)

No. 1. "Review of research on in-service education: a UK perspective", by Professor Michael ERAUT, United Kingdom (doc. DECS/Rech (88) 25)

No. 2. "Efficiency of the further training of teachers and education administrators", by Professor V G ONUSHKIN, USSR (doc. DECS/Rech (88) 78)

No. 3. "Research into the further education of teachers in the German Democratic Republic", by Professor Dr Helmut STOLZ, GDR (doc. DECS/Rech (88) 29)

No. 4. "In-service training of teachers: French research", by Dr Francine BEST and Mrs Monique VIAL, France (doc. DECS/Rech (88) 28)

No. 5. "Suggestopaedia = experimental project Liechtenstein School", by Dr Rudolf BATLINER, Liechtenstein (doc. DECS/Rech (88) 55)

2. INDIVIDUAL OR NATIONAL REPORTS, TABLED AS BACKGROUND MATERIAL

BELGIUM — "In-service training of teachers: the case of the Flemish part of Belgium", by Professor J HEENE (doc. DECS/Rech (88) 81)

— "How can we transform the methods used by serving teachers (towards an in-service training model based on teachers' methods)", by M CRAHAY (doc. DECS/Rech (87) 39)

— "Report mainly concerning the Institute of School Administration of the State University in Mons (Belgium)", by Professor Pol DUPONT (doc. DECS/ Rech (88) 43)

BULGARIA — "The efficiency of long-term supplementary training of teachers and heads of educational institutions in the People's Republic of Bulgaria", by the Bulgarian UNESCO Commission (doc. DECS/Rech (88) 11)

CANADA — "In-service education program for teachers. A Canadian (Province of Ontario) perspective", by Dr G WHITE (doc. DECS/Rech (88) 83)

CYPRUS — "Research on teacher education in Cyprus", by the Pedagogical Institute, Nicosia (DECS/Rech (87) 36)

CZECHOSLOVAKIA — "Improvement of further education of educational administrators", by PhDr Zuzana KOLLARIKOVA (doc. DECS/ Rech (88) 77)

— "In-service education of educational personnel in the Czechoslovak Social-ist Republic", by Dr J LIHOCKY (doc. DECS/Rech (88) 2)

FINLAND — "Trends in in-service and training of teachers and school leaders in Finland", by Dr Sauli TAKALA (doc. DECS/ Rech (88) 24)

FRANCE — "In-service action research training for teachers of English in lower secondary schools", by Nicole BUCHER-POTEAUX (doc. DECS/ Rech (88) 17)

— "La formation des enseignants du premier degré en école normale", by Danielle ZAY (DECS/Rech (88) 62)

— "Effectiveness of in-service education and training of teachers and school leaders — the situation in agricultural education in France", by Michel BOULET (doc. DECS/Rech (88) 51)

— "Initial and in-service training of teachers", by Pierre DELORME (doc. DECS/Rech (88) 58)

FEDERAL REPUBLIC OF GERMANY — "In-service education of school leaders in North Rhine-Westphalia: basic course in organisation development", by Herbert BUCHEN (doc. DECS/Rech (88) 10)

— "In-service teacher education in Berlin (West)", by Schulrat Dr W FEST (doc. DECS/Rech (88) 59)

— "The effectiveness of in-service teacher training and training of school leaders in Bavaria", by Ludwig HARING (doc. DECS/Rech (88) 9)

— "Evaluation of in-service teacher training courses North Rhine-Westphalia", by W MATZKE (doc. DECS/Rech (87) 41)

GERMAN DEMOCRATIC REPUBLIC — "On the implementation of education for peace and international understanding in the scope of in-service teacher training in the German Democratic Republic", by Dr Manfred HAAK (doc. DECS/Rech (88) 75)

— "Use of teaching aids in seminars of in-service training of teachers", by Dr Manfred HAAK (doc. DECS/ Rech (88) 76)

GREECE — "Initial training and in-service training of primary and secondary school teachers: the Greek case", by Yorgos MARKOU (doc. DECS/Rech (88) 79)

HUNGARY — "The effectiveness of INSET in Hungary in the light of some examinations", by Dr Péter SZEBENYI (doc. DECS/Rech (88) 52)

— "Hungarian teachers' views on in-service teacher training" and "An analysis of communication between teachers concerning the major issues of their profession", by Edit TETTAMANTI (doc. DECS/Rech (88) 1)

— "In-service training of teachers (1985-1988) selected annotated bibliography covering literature in the Hungarian language", by Ferenc DEAK (doc. DECS/Rech (88) 48)

IRELAND — "In-service teacher education in Ireland", by Dr Thomas KELLAGHAN (doc. DECS/Rech (88) 33)

ITALY — "In-service education and training of teachers and school leaders — Bibliographical Notes" by Dr Paolo DALESSANDRO (doc. DECS/Rech (88) 56)

LIECHTENSTEIN — "Education in Liechtenstein", by the Schools' Office, Vaduz (doc. DECS/Rech (88) 16)

NETHERLANDS — "Utilization and research programming: major concerns of educational policy oriented research for the 80s", by Dr J G LODEWIJKS (doc. DECS/Rech (88) 43)

NORWAY — "Milieu and leadership in the school — A Norwegian INSET project without goal attainment" by Kari JOHANSEN and Arild TJELDVOLL (doc. DECS/Rech (88) 19)

POLAND — "The in-service training of teachers as a realisation of the idea of permanent education" by Professor Stanislaw KACZOR (doc. DECS/Rech (88) 49)

— "Research activities in Poland" by the European Information Centre for Further Education of Teachers, Prague (doc. DECS/Rech (88) 18)

PORTUGAL — "Teacher training programs: some results from national surveys in Portugal" by Maria do CARMO CLIMACO (doc. DECS/Rech (88) 74)

— "Consideration on the organisation of an INSET system in Portugal" by Professor Manuel Ferreira PATRICIO (doc. DECS/Rech (88) 84)

SAN MARINO — "The laws, the structure and the organisation of the Sanmarinese School System" by Carla NICOLINI and Filiberto BERNARDI (doc. DECS/Rech (88) 85)

SWITZERLAND — "Research activities in Switzerland" by the Federal Office of Education and Science, Berne (doc. DECS/Rech (88) 34)

— "Research work and bibliography" by Dr Willy JEANNERET (doc. DECS/Rech (88) 57)

UKRAINE — "In-service training of school leavers", by Dr GOUDZ (doc. DECS/Rech (88) 54)

— "Research into the problems of in-service teacher training", by Dr A SIROTENKO (doc. DECS/Rech (88) 53)

UNITED KINGDOM — "Current research projects into INSET being undertaken by the London University Institute of Education", by Professor Guy NEAVE (doc. DECS/Rech (88) 65)

YUGOSLAVIA — "Drama workshops as a means of pre-school teacher training", by Mirjana PESIC (doc. DECS/Rech (88) 40)

OTHER BACKGROUND PAPERS

List of ongoing completed research (Part 1) compiled by the Secretariat of the Documentation Section, Directorate of Education, Culture and Sport, on the basis of national contributions (doc. DECS/Rech (87) 45)

Current research projects in Hungary and Czechoslovakia, by the European Information Centre of Charles University for Further Education of Teachers (doc. DECS/Rech (88) 31)

Bibliography, compiled by Jitka HRADILOVÁ and Anna SOUCKOVÁ (doc. DECS/Rech (88) 50)

Bibliography, compiled by Ursula GIERE and Imke BEHR (doc. DECS/Rech (88) 35)

Bibliography, compiled by the Secretariat (Documentation Section, Directorate of Education, Culture and Sport) (doc. DECS/Rech (87) 44)

"In-service training of teachers in the 80s", by PhDr Marie ČERNÁ, CSc. (doc. DECS/Rech (88) 45)

"In-service training of teachers, issues and trends", by Dr Svatopluk PETRÁČEK (doc. DECS/Rech (87) 25)

"Comparative analysis of the information process in the field of in-service training of educational personnel", by PhDr Hana PROCHÁZKOVÁ, PhDr Jitka HRADILOVÁ and PhDr Anna SOUČKOVÁ (doc. DECS/Rech (88) 44)

EUROPEAN MEETINGS ON EDUCATIONAL RESEARCH

Part A

The Educational Research Symposia, Colloquies, and Workshops are initiated by the Council of Europe Council for Cultural Cooperation (CCC).

This series educational research meetings take place since 1975 and bring together research workers from the different member countries to discuss educational problems in order to provide Ministries of Education with research findings in which they might base their policy decisions. Cooperation should also lead to a joint European evaluation of certain educational reforms and developments.

C. Harrison (Ed.)

Interactive Learning and the New Technologies

Report of the Educational Research Workshop organised under the auspices of the Council of Europe, Eindhoven, the Netherlands, 1987.

The theme 'interactive learning and the new technologies' was chosen because of the growing importance of the new technologies both in education and the labour market. The idea was to bring together research and experience showing in what ways the new technologies had succeeded or can be successful to promote classroom innovation through interactive learning.

1988, 192 pp., ISBN 90 265 0969 3, hardbound.

In the USA and Canada available from:
Taylor & Francis Inc. International Publishers
1900 Frost Road, Suite 101, Bristol, PA 19007, USA
Telephone (215) 785 5800

Also available from your bookseller.

SWETS & ZEITLINGER B.V.   PUBLISHERS
                                          PUBLISHING SERVICE

Heereweg 347, 2161 CA, Lisse, The Netherlands, Telephone 02521-35111

EUROPEAN MEETINGS ON EDUCATIONAL RESEARCH

Part B

European Conferences of Directors of Educational Research Institutions organised in cooperation with UNESCO, the UNESCO Institute for Education in Hamburg, and the Council of Europe Council for Cultural Cooperation (CCC).

The papers of these meetings are published as a book so that ministries and interested reseach workers, as well as a wider public (teachers, parents, media) are kept informed of the present state of research at a European level.

A. McAlpine, S. Brown, S. Lang & E. Kentley (Eds.)

New Challenges for Teachers and Teacher Education

Report of the Fourth All-European Conference of Directors of Educational Research Institutions organised in cooperation with the UNESCO Institute for Education in Hamburg and the Council of Europe Council for Cultural Co-operation, Hungary, 1986.

The theme of this conference 'new challenges for teachers and teacher education with special reference to the functions and organisation of the school' reflects current priorities of the most European countries.

1988, 180 pp, ISBN 90 265 0884 0, hardbound.

In the USA and Canada available from:
Taylor & Francis Inc. International Publishers
1900 Frost Road, Suite 101
Bristol, PA 19007, USA
Telephone (215) 785 5800

Also available from your bookseller.

SWETS & ZEITLINGER B.V.   PUBLISHERS
                                    PUBLISHING SERVICE

Heereweg 347, 2161 CA, Lisse, The Netherlands, Telephone 02521-35111

Other titles published in Part B:

Educational Research in Europe

M. Dino Carelli & Peter Sachsenmeier (Eds.)
Report of the First All-European Conference for Directors of Educational
Research Institutions, Hamburg, Federal Republic of Germany, 1976.
The theme of the conference was 'the impact of educational research on
school reform'. It was discussed from the point of view of national,
institutional and project levels.
1977.   148 pp.   ISBN 90 265 0250 8

A New Look at the Relationship between
School Education and Work

M. Dino Carelli (Ed.)
Report of the Second All-European Conference for Directors of Educational
Research Institutions, Madrid, Spain, 1979.
Training schemes and work education programmes no longer seem to suit
the present-day job market. The relationship between education and work
and the methods of training needs to be redefined. Research in the field of
education for work will be increasing as a consequence. This conference was
organised in order to identify the available research and the areas where
further research is needed.
1980.   170 pp.   ISBN 90 265 0355 5

Research into Primary Education

The Secretariat of the Council of Europe (Ed.)
Report of the Third All-European Conference for Directors of Educational
Research Institutions, Neusiedl, Austria, 1983.
What do society, the state, and the parents expect from primary education?
What is the situation of the child (5-10 years) in primary school? Three
aspects were discussed: 1. Aims and objectives of primary education. 2. The
situation of primary school children in modern society. 3. The organisation
and methods of primary education.
1985.   212 pp.   ISBN 90 265 0616 3

In the USA and Canada available from Taylor & Francis Inc. International Publishers
1900 Frost Road, Suite 101, Bristol, PA 19007, USA   Telephone (215) 785 5800
Also available from your bookseller.

SWETS & ZEITLINGER B.V.   PUBLISHERS

PUBLISHING SERVICE

Heereweg 347, 2161 CA, Lisse, The Netherlands, Telephone 02521-35111

W. Tomic & P.C. van der Sijde

Changing Teaching for Better Learning

What is it that teachers do that leads to student learning? How can we increase students' achievement and improve their attitudes? In order to improve the quality of education the authors focus on teaching/learning processes taking place in the traditional classroom situations. The study reported is the Dutch contribution to the IEA Classroom Environment Study: Teaching for Learning, whose general objective is to identify alterable teaching behaviors that correlate with desirable cognitive and affective student learning outcomes, and to develop a training program that will recommend ways of organizing teaching/learning processes. Results show that even a short training course can successfully change the teachers' teaching script, and, subsequently their teaching behavior, which in turn influences student achievement.

1989, 124 pp., ISBN 90 265 1019 5

In the USA and Canada available from:
Taylor & Francis Inc. International Publishers
1900 Frost Road, Suite 101
Bristol, PA 19007, USA
Telephone (215) 785 5800

Also available from your bookseller.

SWETS & ZEITLINGER B.V.   PUBLISHERS
PUBLISHING SERVICE

Heereweg 347, 2161 CA, Lisse, The Netherlands, Telephone 02521-35111

J.J. Beishuizen. J. Tobin & P.R. Weston (Eds.)

The Use of the Microcomputer in Teaching and Learning

This Unesco Joint Study No. 3 focuses its attention on three major changes to be expected from the introduction and use of information technology in education.
1. Changes in the teaching and learning processes.
2. Changes in the role of the teacher and the learner.
3. Changes in the curriculum.
This book presents experiences from the participating countries which were considered relevant with respect to the three perspectives or changes to be expected in education.
The second part of the book is a collection of eleven case studies reported by teachers, regional administrators, managers of international programmes, and researchers in the area of education and information technology.

1988, 272 pp., ISBN 90 265 0894 8, hardbound.

In the USA and Canada available from:
Taylor & Francis Inc. International Publishers
1900 Frost Road, Suite 101
Bristol, PA 19007, USA
Telephone (215) 785 5800

Also available from your bookseller.

SWETS & ZEITLINGER B.V.   PUBLISHERS
                                                PUBLISHING SERVICE

Heereweg 347, 2161 CA, Lisse, The Netherlands, Telephone 02521-35111

J.T. Voorbach & L.G.M. Prick

TEACHER EDUCATION 5
Research and Developments on Teacher Education in the Netherlands

This fifth volume in the series TEACHER EDUCATION contains
almost all the Dutch contributions to the annual conference of the
Association for Teacher Education in Europe (ATEE), held in Spain
(1988). The theme of this conference was 'The development of teachers
in a changing society'.
This volume offers a quite complete overview of the research and up-to-
date developments on teacher education in the Netherlands. All articles
have been reviewed by experts in the field of teacher education. The
contributions are arranged to various themes that are of influence on the
content, structure and organization of pre-service and in-service teacher
education, e.g. emancipation, technology, management, methodology,
evaluation, subjective theories, the development of the teacher.

1989, 204 pp., ISBN 90 6472 150 5

In the USA and Canada available from:
Taylor & Francis Inc. International Publishers
1900 Frost Road, Suite 101
Bristol, PA 19007, USA
Telephone (215) 785 5800

Also available from your bookseller.

SWETS & ZEITLINGER B.V.   PUBLISHERS
PUBLISHING SERVICE

Heereweg 347, 2161 CA, Lisse, The Netherlands, Telephone 02521-35111